JOINING THE ARMY THAT SHEDS NO BLOOD

JOINING THE ARMY THAT SHEDS NO BLOOD

Susan Clemmer Steiner

Foreword by Richard A. Kauffman
Cartoons by Joel Kauffmann

A Christian Peace Shelf Selection

HERALD PRESS
Waterloo, Ontario
Scottdale, Pennsylvania

146736

Canadian Cataloguing in Publication Data

Steiner, Susan Clemmer, 1947-
    Joining the army that sheds no blood

(A Christian Peace shelf selection)
Includes index.
ISBN 0-8361-3305-6

1. Peace (Theology) - Biblical teaching.
2. Jesus Christ-Teachings.   I. Title.   II. Series.

BT736.4.S73   261.8'73   C82-094490-4

The paper used in this publication is recycled and
meets the minimum requirements of American National
Standard for Information Sciences—Permanence of Paper
for Printed Library Materials, ANSI Z39.48-1984.

JOINING THE ARMY THAT SHEDS NO BLOOD
Copyright © 1982, 1991 by Herald Press, Waterloo, Ont.
N2L 6H7.
    Published simultaneously in the United States by
    Herald Press, Scottdale, Pa. 15683. All rights reserved.
Library of Congress Catalog Card Number: 82-81510
International Standard Book Number: 0-8361-3305-6
Printed in the United States of America

99 98 97 96 95 94 93 92 91 10 9 8 7 6 5 4 3 2

For
Mom and Dad Clemmer
and
Mom and Dad Steiner

They passed on to us the tradition of
Christian peacemaking which
they had received.
Now I pass it on to you,
the reader.

Contents

Foreword

I sit before my TV, intrigued by a commercial. The sales pitch is enticing, the music catchy, and the rhythm hypnotic: "Be all that you can be, 'cause we need you in the Army.... We don't ask for experience, we give it! The Army, the Navy, the Air Force, the Marines." The commercial offers young people adventure, job training, experience—even a college education. But deceptively absent from this mesmerizing sales pitch is any suggestion that the purpose of the military is to fight and kill and make war.

In this book, the author speaks of another kind of army, one that sheds no blood. This army is committed to peace, not war; the creative resolution of conflict, not the violent clash of opposing parties; the effort to make friends of enemies instead of making mincemeat of them.

If Sue Clemmer Steiner's book had been available when I was a teenager, it might have helped me make up my mind about how peace relates to Christian faith. It would have answered some of the questions I had then. Why do some Christians justify participation in the military and in war and others do not? Didn't God command wars in the Old Testament? Why did he change his mind about war if, in fact, he did? Jesus preached peace, true, but didn't he use force to drive the moneychangers from the temple? And what about godless communism? Is it not an international menace which must be contained for the sake of the gospel? These were just some of the questions I had then.

When I was in my mid-teens, one Sunday morning I was herded into a room with other fellows to talk about our "decision." Facing registration with the Selective Service System at age eighteen, we had to make up our minds whether to register as conscientious objectors. The pastor was there to remind us that we were from a peace church. Going to war is wrong, our tradition had concluded long ago.

I left that meeting feeling that my church considered going into the army as wrong, but since it was my choice, the impression was almost left that peacemaking was optional for the Christian. That obviously wasn't what the pastor intended to convey. But because peace was talked about in so few other settings in congregational life, my reading of the situation might have been legitimate. Why was the church's stance on peace such a secretive matter that we had to be called together for a special session to talk about it—almost as if we were there to talk about sex!

Sometimes I have had to conclude that the message of peace is the church's best-kept secret, even in the so-called historic peace churches. *Joining the Army That Sheds No Blood* helps unveil that secret and explain the conviction of a growing number of Christians that the way of Jesus is the way of peace. This book strikes a good balance between examining what the Bible has to say on the subject and applying biblical teaching to issues facing Christians today. And it is easy and fun to read.

Joining the Army That Sheds No Blood is a call to battle, not to wage war but to wage peace. To join this army or not to join it is a decision all of us have to make. This book will help you decide as a Christian on one of the most important issues in your life.

Richard A. Kauffman
Mennonite Publishing House
Scottdale, Pennsylvania

Invitation to the Reader

This book is an introduction to a very special group—the army that sheds no blood.

But maybe armies don't interest you. Maybe you'd rather play in an orchestra or march in a parade. Maybe you'd rather plant some seeds and watch them grow.

If that's the case, this book is for you too. Because the army, the orchestra, and the seed planters all refer to the same thing—a great company of Christian peacemakers. And you're invited to join.

While this group has always been a minority, it's larger than you might think. I happen to be Mennonite—a member of one of the historic peace churches. But if you're from another church, please don't stop reading. We're only a small part of the whole, and we need your perspective.

Actually, Christians from every denomination, every country, every century, and every imaginable political system have belonged to the army of Christian peacemakers. It's an active group—not one that sits around and does nothing. Yet the kind of action it takes and the effect it has baffles many people.

If we're going to be well-grounded Christian peacemakers, we'll have to think through some things carefully. That's the reason for this book.

So first, we'll look at what's wrong with our world as it is. Secondly, we'll explore how Jesus shows (and is) the way to peace. Next, we'll make the connection between Jesus and ourselves as members of the army that sheds no blood.

After that comes the hardest part. We'll have to seriously consider three arguments against Christian peacemaking which all of us will encounter sometime. Then finally, in the last two chapters, we'll summarize what Christian peacemakers do and the beliefs which undergird our actions.

In the book, you'll find my paraphrases of quite a few Bible passages. Naturally, they're the ones Christian peacemakers and their opponents argue about. The Bible references are given so you can look them up for yourself.

Since this book focuses on the question of war, it talks specifically about pacifism. A pacifist—or conscientious objector—demonstrates his or her beliefs about peacemaking by not participating in the military. But you'll soon see (if you don't know already) that pacifism is just the beginning for Christian peacemakers.

Lots of people bolstered my courage as I wrote this book. Nine adult peacemakers—Conrad Brunk, J. R. Burkholder, Jesse Glick, Walter Klaassen, Ernie Regehr, John Rempel, Hubert Schwartzentruber, John Stoner, and Marvin Warkentin—read the whole thing and made helpful suggestions. So did two teenage friends—Paul Bast and Beth Brubacher.

Conrad Grebel College gave me an office and coffee—two essentials for any writer!

I also want to mention two teachers, Helen Lapp and Dan Hess. They helped me believe in myself as a writer way back in high school and college.

Finally, there's my husband Sam. His pacifism brought me to Canada in 1969, and his love and support brought me through this project now.

Susan Clemmer Steiner
August 2, 1981

Getting Our Bearings

Imagine for a moment that we're on a spaceship. We've been travelling in outer space and are now passing near Planet Earth. We see mountains and oceans and plains.

But—oh—what's this coming up now? It looks like a small mountain range, but not quite. Could it be—it must be—it *is* the Great Wall of China. It's not as old as the mountains and oceans; it's pretty old, nonetheless—2200 years old, to be exact. It's the only thing made by those Earthlings which we can see from out here. It must be a monument of some sort.

Oh, yes, I remember now. An Earthling told me about it once. It's a national security system, built to keep out the Huns. (They got in anyway, but that's another story.)

But, speaking of security systems, have you seen all those

satellites orbiting Planet Earth these days? They're a menace for travellers like us! They mostly belong to two big countries in the northern hemisphere called the United States and the Soviet Union, who spy on each other however they can. A country called Canada lies between them. It's hooked up with the American spy network.

I'm told that North Americans are big on something called "science fiction." They like to watch TV programs and movies about wars carried on in space. In other words, they enjoy dreams and nightmares about possibilities their technology isn't quite up to yet.

But they're getting there. They have a new program called the "space shuttle" now, and there's talk of zapping each other's missiles with "killer satellites." If *Star Wars* becomes science fact, we'll *really* have to watch out for those Earthlings.

I can't figure it out, but for some reason those Earthlings are obsessed with security systems. I hear that the United States has enough missiles pointed at the Soviet Union (USSR) to kill people 40 times over, and the USSR has enough missiles pointed at the United States to kill people 26 times over. They call this arrangement Mutually Assured Destruction. (But if you know the Earthling language called English, you can see that it's just plain MAD.)

They tell me that the United States and the USSR and their buddies also have a new system called "war by proxy." What happens is that countries in the northern hemisphere sell

arms to countries in the southern hemisphere who will protect their interests. Then they let the natives slug it out. Since 1955, there've been 130 wars on Planet Earth—most of them in the southern hemisphere.

Also, an Earthling once told me that on his planet, they spend $1 million every minute on military forces and weapons. Half of their engineers and scientists work on military projects.

Do you think that's why those brainy North Americans can't design a decent pollution control device for their cars or keep a decent railway system functioning? You can't solve *every* problem at once, now can you? You have to set some priorities.

Those Earthlings—I wonder what happened to them, anyway? They're a menace to themselves and to the rest of us out here. Surely the God of the universe didn't want things to turn out quite like *this*. I wonder what happened.

PONTIUS' PUDDLE

SNOW IS LIKE THE NEW YEAR. IT BEGINS AS A GIFT FROM GOD--

PURE, UNSPOILED, FULL OF HOPE AND PROMISE.

SPLAT

THEN IT FALLS INTO THE HANDS OF MANKIND.

JOINING THE ARMY THAT SHEDS NO BLOOD

1
Peace, Peace: If God Wants It, Why Isn't There Any?

War is the devil's joke on humanity.
        —William Allen White.

Our world seems programmed wrong.

In the 1960's, a black American revolutionary named Rap Brown upset a lot of people when he said, "Violence is as American as cherry pie." He wasn't trying to be funny, either.

In sleepy towns across North America, little old ladies (and men) have flower boxes stolen from their front porches; to feel safe, they doublelock their doors at night.

Many citizens think owning a gun will make them feel safer. In Cleveland not long ago, neighbors found an old man named Mr. Wesley dead in his bed, surrounded by rifles, pistols, and guns. A harpoon was even propped against the fridge! But the fridge was empty. Mr. Wesley had spent his Social Security and pension checks on guns—and starved to death.

And then, of course, there's the Mutually Assured Destruction (MAD) policy of the superpowers. The idea is that if one country attacks another with nuclear weapons, the country attacked will unleash nuclear weapons sufficient to obliterate the attacking country.

There's the way our ancestors settled the North American continent at the expense of the native peoples. And all those assassination attempts on presidents, prophets, and popes.

But before we blame the programmer of the universe for all this, let's go back to the beginning. The Hebrew writers in Genesis 1 and 2 give us two slightly different but compatible pictures of what God had in mind for human beings and for Planet Earth.

The Composer, the Symphony, and the Orchestra
(Genesis 1 and 2)

"Well," said God, "that part of the job is done. I've made the earth and put life on it in an orderly way—human life even.

"Just by looking at our world, you can see that everything has a purpose. I've made you human beings for a purpose. I've made you in my image so you'll know how to look after the planet for me.

"That means . . . it sort of means that I'm the director of the play and you're the actors. Or, I'm the composer of a new symphony, and you're members of the orchestra. I have a plan for this new symphony, and it's beautiful. In fact, it's perfect. Your job is to work out the music. It's music full of peace and harmony. Peace—what do I mean by peace?

"I don't just mean the absence of war, or anything like that. I mean positive well-being. I mean . . . picture a garden. Think of a cool garden on a hot summer day. Think of a river in the garden which waters the trees. The trees look luscious and their fruit is good to eat. That's what I mean by positive well-being, by peace and harmony.

"I'm teaching you this beautiful music—the music of life, the music of the universe—so you can take care of the garden for me. Since I'm the composer, I won't even be around a lot of the time. Our symphony has some difficult spots—some really stunning parts, in fact—so you'll have to work hard. But you can do it. After all, you're made in my image.

"But whatever you do—don't try to rewrite the music. You'll ruin it if you do. The music as it is enables you to preserve and develop the world I've given you."

The Devil's Joke Begins
(Genesis 3)

This all sounds very good. So, what happened? What went wrong? One way to put it is that the devil played an enormous joke on humanity.

But, wait a minute. Maybe it's easier to understand if we picture just one man (named Adam) and one woman (named Eve) who hold the promise of all humanity. Then our story goes something like this. . . .

Suddenly Eve had an idea. The power of suggestion came from somewhere inside or outside of herself and she thought:

"Hey, there's one place where this music just doesn't sound right to me. I think the composer must have gotten it wrong. I'll try a different run and see what happens. There's no reason why I can't write music.

"Hey, Adam, listen to this! Don't you think it's better than what the composer gave us?"

Adam tried the new run. He liked it too. He tinkered around some more, and decided he'd make a pretty good composer.

So Adam and Eve practiced for awhile in the garden, adding their own variations from time to time. But suddenly, they saw something they hadn't before. They realized they were stark naked.

Adam looked at Eve and thought, "O my, she can see me exactly as I am."

Eve looked at Adam and thought, "O my, he can see me exactly as I am."

Then Adam looked at himself and an even worse thought occurred to him. "O my, I can see *myself* exactly as I am." Eve looked at herself and thought the same thing.

Somehow, all this had never bothered them before. But now it did. So they found some fig leaves and hid behind them.

The Composer Comes Back

Then—horror of horrors—the composer came back onstage. Adam and Eve stopped playing and ran for cover. Somehow they knew that the symphony was already ruined.

First, God had to fish them out of the bushes. "We are naked," said Adam. "We have no defenses—from ourselves or each other or you. We have to cover up. We have to hide."

"So," said God, "that's honest enough so far. But tell me, Adam, why did you try to change the music?"

"Well, actually," said Adam, pointing a finger at Eve, "it was all *her* idea." He had never tried to push anything off on Eve before. He had never had to.

"And you, Eve?" God asked. "What about you?"

"Well, ah, it was the power of suggestion. That snake there . . . it was *his* idea . . . the devil made me do it!"

"I see," said God to himself. "They're all blaming somebody else. Nobody wants to take responsibility for his or her own actions."

To Adam and Eve he said, "Well, as you can see, the garden is gone. The harmony, the sense of well-being—it's gone. It's left as a memory of what was possible and as a vision for the future—but for now, it's gone.

"You didn't like my version of security. You thought you could compose a better symphony. Well, go to it.

You're *really* on your own now. I still care about you, and I'll try to help you. But, as I said, the garden is *gone*. So you may as well leave."

I Don't Have a Brother
(Genesis 4)

The story of Adam and Eve is the story of *us*—the story of humanity. The story that follows right after it is a story about us too. It's called "I Don't Have a Brother," and it goes like this:

Adam and Eve, being a man and a woman, eventually had two sons named Cain and Abel.

When they grew up, both Cain and Abel brought an offering to God. For some reason, God accepted Abel's offering but not Cain's.

Cain desperately wanted something Abel had—God's blessing. Instead of trying to figure out what the problem was (as God suggested he should do), Cain took it out on his brother. He was jealous, angry, and insecure, so he killed his brother. He made his brother into "the enemy."

Then God came to Cain and said, "Tell me, Cain, where's your brother?"

And Cain answered, "Who, Abel? Oh, him . . . I'm not responsible for him. In fact, I don't even *have* a brother."

"O my," said God. "Until you can start taking responsibility for yourself and others, you're going to be a fugitive. Wherever you go, you'll still be a wanderer inside yourself. You'll keep looking for security, but you won't be able to find it."

Cain Without the Eye Contact

War happens when the simple situations of the Adam and Eve story and the Cain and Abel story play themselves out on a large scale by groups of people in nations and in alliances of nations.

War is—at least in one sense—murder on a large scale. It happens when we don't see that the people we're refusing to be responsible for are really our brothers and sisters.

A nineteenth-century American pacifist named Henry Wright said:

> Let all soldiers and all advocates of war be told that they are murderers . . . and let the truth be brought home to them on all occasions, till they feel its force, and then, and not till then, will men learn and advocate war no more.

It's pretty hard to take away life when you're looking into another person's eyes. But the weapons' systems of the 1980's enable us to avoid any possible "eye contact" with the victims of our wars. On a CBS-TV special, a young technician at a U.S. missile command post said:

> I wonder sometimes about the people at the other end. I'm glad I don't know the targets. I might become kind of emotional about the people I'd be destroying.

Do Stereos and Designer Jeans Cause Wars?
(James 4:1-2)

John Woolman, an eighteenth-century American Quaker businessman, suggested that we need to "look upon our treasures, the furniture of our houses and our garments, and see whether the seeds of war have nourishment in these our possessions."

In other words, Woolman is asking whether it's possible that our stereos, hot cars, and designer jeans contribute to causing wars in our world today.

Our first reaction is to say, "Now really! This man can't be serious!"

But Woolman didn't just pull this idea out of the air somewhere. He's echoing a couple verses from the book of James, in which the author asks a question and answers it himself:

> Where do all the fights and quarrels among you come from? They come from your desires for pleasure, which are constantly fighting within you. You want things, but you cannot have them, so you are ready to kill; you strongly desire things, but you cannot get them, so you quarrel and fight. (TEV)

"Now wait a minute, James!" I can hear us all protesting. "Of course we like our stereos and cars and designer jeans. But we're not about to go out and kill somebody to get them. We're not *that* greedy!"

No, of course not. But maybe stereos and a car for everybody and designer jeans are symbols of our North American way of life. There are certain things we expect, just because we're North Americans. Without even thinking about it, we all just expect that our country will be greedy for us.

Bananas on the Cereal, Sugar in the Pop

We just expect that we can have bananas on our cereal and sugar in our pop (unless we're drinking that horrid diet stuff). In a few years, most of us will be addicted to coffee (if we're not already). We just expect to have bananas, sugar, and coffee, and we don't think we ought to pay a fortune for them.

We just expect to have gasoline in our tanks, and we don't want to pay a fortune for it, either. In fact, we *need* gasoline and all the other oil products, since our whole way of life runs on oil. We just assume our countries will do their part to make sure it keeps flowing.

We also *need* scarce metals of various kinds. Take cobalt, for example. We need it to treat cancer patients. We also need it to build jet engines and nuclear propulsion systems.

Without even thinking about it, we expect sugar and

oil and cobalt. We almost assume that these natural resources—many of them from the southern hemisphere—are ours by right, We're not nasty people. We just don't think about it.

We don't think about what we might be asking our countries to do to get them for us. We don't think about the fact that skirmishes in Latin America or Africa can easily escalate because of the arms our countries have sold to the locals to protect our interests. We don't think about the fact that a lot of those 130 wars since World War II are involved with protecting resources for us in the northern hemisphere.

The Case of the Katangese Rebels

Take, for example, the central African country of Zaire, which used to be called the Belgian Congo. After the Congo won its independence in 1960, fighting continued between various ethnic groups. The mineral-rich southern province of Katanga seceded for awhile. But eventually the Katangese tribesmen "lost" and were forced to flee to neighboring Angola.

During the 1970's, the cobalt located in Katangese territory (now called Shaba Province) became increasingly important on the world market. Sixty-six percent of the cobalt traded in the world comes from Zaire, and it's very high-grade stuff. Most of it goes to NATO countries, especially the United States and France. These same countries supply Zaire with most of its arms.

In 1978, some of the exiled Katangese launched an attack from across the border in Angola to get their ancestral land back. This really upset the NATO countries. If there were prolonged fighting in Shaba Province, NATO access to the cobalt would be endangered. The world price of cobalt shot up from $50 to $685/lb.

What made people nervous was that Angola (where

the Katangese had taken refuge) was now a communist country. Everybody was afraid that if the Katangese took control of their ancestral land again, they might want to sell the cobalt to the USSR.

We in North America were told that France had to go into Zaire with troops to "throw the Communists out" (with some United States military equipment and Belgian troops on the scene as well). But we were only told part of the story. The part about the United States and France trying to protect "our cobalt" was left out.

If the Katangese ancestral land had been a desert area with no minerals, the United States and France would have let the African ethnic groups slug it out themselves.

From a Garden to a City
(Revelation 21)

The garden is gone. The symphony has really taken a disastrous turn.

We live in a world where far-off peoples become enemies if they threaten our sources of bananas, oil, and metals; a world where out of fear and suspicion, the superpowers have enough missiles aimed at each other to kill us all many times over; a world where many countries have large military bureaucracies paid to think about war every day, to plan for it, and to develop scenarios for winning.

Is this the way it has to go on and on? Is this all the God of the universe can promise us?

It just so happens that the Bible ends as it begins— with a picture of peace. The picture of peace in the book of Revelation isn't a garden, but rather a city.

In this city, someone called the Lamb provides the light. The nations live by this light, and the rulers of the world bring their riches (natural resources?!) into the city. There's no security problem, so the gates to the city are never shut. People can come and go as they wish.

The gap between our world and that city seems almost impossible to bridge. Maybe that's one reason it's called a "vision"! A lot of attitudes would have to change for such a picture of peace to become reality.

The key to the vision and the reality is found in this someone called the Lamb. That's why we're going to spend the next three chapters considering him. We're talking, of course, about Jesus.

Ain't Gonna Study War No More
(Isaiah 2:4; Micah 4:3, 4)

Jesus is the Bible's most important signpost to peace. He ties together the picture of positive well-being at the beginning of the Bible with the one at the end.

But, wait a minute. There's another important picture of peace in the Bible too! It pops up right in the middle, in the writings of the Hebrew prophets Isaiah and Micah in the eighth century B.C. It looks like this:

> He [God] will wield authority over many peoples and arbitrate for mighty nations;
> they will hammer their swords into plowshares, their spears into sickles.
> Nation will not lift sword against nation, there will be no more training for war.

Each man will sit under his vine and his fig tree, with no one to trouble him (JB).

A main feature of this picture of peace is that "there will be no more training for war." Or, as the Revised Standard Version puts it: "neither shall they learn war anymore." Is there a time coming when nations will "stop learning war"? That seems just about as unreal—as incompatible with everything we know about our world—as the city at the end of Revelation does. So many Christians call this a "vision" of peace and leave it at that.

But many other Christians throughout the ages have decided there's one thing they *can* do to help move this vision of peace closer to reality. That is, they can personally "hammer their swords into plowshares" and encourage others to do the same. They can say, along with the composers of a familiar Negro spiritual, "I ain't gonna study war no more."

Now if it were as simple as all that, we could stop right here. But it's not simple at all. A lot of questions come tumbling out. Questions like:

"What good can it do for *me* to 'stop studying war'? It seems like hardly a drop in the bucket."

OR, "If the world stayed as it is, and all Canadians

and Americans *did* stop studying war, what would happen to us? We have to remember the Russians, after all."

OR, "How do we even know that God wants us to do this? I mean, the Bible says different things at different places."

OR, "If everything is as complex as you say it is, with our countries going after oil and metals which we expect without even knowing it, then how is it even possible for us to stop studying war if we want to?"

These are difficult questions. Finding our way through them will be a real struggle. But I think we're up to it. So read on. . . .

We'll start by considering Jesus, since he's the key to peace.

Review and Reflect

1. What do you think of the statement that "war is the devil's joke on humanity"? Do you agree with this chapter that war is rooted in human sin and greed?

2. Read for yourself the three biblical pictures of peace discussed in this chapter (Genesis 1-2; Micah 4; Revelation 21). If you were to create your own vision of positive well-being, what would it be like?

3. React to this quote from *Eternity* magazine: "There are but a few things on earth worth dying for. Oil is not one of them."

4. What do you expect your country to do to keep our standard of living the way it is?

5. Way back in 1953, President Eisenhower said:

   Every gun that is made, every warship launched, every rocket fired signifies, in the final sense, a theft from those who hunger and are not fed. . . . The world in arms is not spending money alone. It is spending the sweat of its laborers, the genius of its scientists, the hopes of its children. . . . This is not a way of life at all, in any true sense.

What do you think?

Books for (Very) Serious Study

Eller, Vernard. *War and Peace from Genesis to Revelation.* Scottdale: Herald Press, 1981. Chapter 1.

Lord, Charlie. *The Rule of the Sword.* Newton: Faith and Life Press, 1978.

Regehr, Ernie. *Militarism and the World Military Order: A Study Guide for Churches.* New York: World Council of Churches, 1980.

Shelly, Maynard. *New Call for Peacemakers.* Newton: Faith and Life Press, 1979. Chapters 1-3.

2
What Jesus Said About Enemies

You have heard that it was said, *"You shall love your neighbor and hate your enemy." But I say to you, "Love your enemies."*

—*Jesus.*

Do I not destroy my enemy when I make him my friend?
—*Abraham Lincoln.*

Most people think there's only one sure way to get rid of an enemy—kill him off!

But in the first century A.D. a teacher came on the scene who advocated another way.

Since he was a Jew, this teacher was well-trained in the Old Testament scriptures. He knew the Ten Commandments, including, "You shall not kill." He knew that its first hearers had taken the commandment to mean, "You shall not murder a fellow Hebrew." That was fine as far as it went, the teacher thought. But did it go far enough?

He also knew about the timeworn principle of "an eye for an eye and a tooth for a tooth." That principle had served people well, he thought. It kept retribution in hand. It meant that people could not say, "If you bomb us, we'll obliterate you. If you bomb a little city, we'll annihilate a whole nation." But again, he wondered if it went far enough.

So the teacher reflected on these two command-ments and on the other 611 laws he had learned. And, like all good teachers, he decided that the only way to make sense of all this material was to summarize it for his students (who were called "disciples").

"It's all very simple," he said when people asked. "All you need to do is *love God* and *love your neighbor.*" Actually, this summary of the Law wasn't even very original. The *love God* part came from Deuteronomy 6:5 and the *love your neighbor* part from Leviticus 19:18.

But what the teacher did with this summary—the way he chose to apply it—was something new. It amounted to a new way of dealing with enemies.

The Story of the Good Mexican
(Luke 10:25-37)

There was a know-it-all college student in California who came up to Jesus and said, "Teacher, what do I have to do to be saved?"

And Jesus answered him, "Well, what does the Bible say? The Old Testament, for instance?"

And the college kid answered, "You're supposed to love God with everything you've got—with your intellect, your body, your heart, and soul. And you're supposed to love your neighbor in the same way that you love your-self."

"You're certainly a smart fellow," said Jesus. "All those years of Sunday school must have done you some good. Follow what you've just said, and you have it made."

"Okay," said the college student. "But just exactly who is my neighbor?"

"Are you sure you really want to know?" asked Jesus. "Let me tell you a story. . . ."

"A man was driving from Bakersfield to Fresno late one night, when another car forced him off the road. Two thugs stole his wallet with all his money, beat him up, and took off with his car.

"First, a famous TV preacher whizzed by the scene of the crime. As his lights beamed at the edge of the highway, he thought he saw a human form huddled there.

" 'My eyes must be playing tricks on me,' he said to himself. 'I've been in front of TV cameras too long.'

"But just to make sure, he told his driver to step on the gas.

"Next, a church youth group president came driving by. Out of the corner of her eye she caught a glimpse of something in the beam of the headlight. But it was late, her boyfriend was driving, and she had to go home and prepare a talk on 'Loving your neighbor' for a youth meeting the next night. So she didn't say anything to her boyfriend.

"Finally, a man in a rusty old van came by. He was a grape picker—a Mexican actually—and he might not even have been able to produce the right immigration papers in a pinch. His English wasn't very good, either.

"But he stopped the van, put the injured man in, and drove off to the local clinic. He paid the standard fee, and waited around till the intern told him the man would recover. He stopped in again the next day, just to make sure everything was okay.

"Now tell me," said Jesus to the college student, "which one of these three was neighbor to the man who was robbed?"

"Uh, well ... I guess it must have been the Mex ... [he couldn't quite bring himself to say it] ... uh ... it was the one who showed love-in-action," said the student.

"Well then," said Jesus, "you go and act the same way."

When Jesus first told the story of the Good Samaritan, his hearers weren't too pleased. In fact, they were shocked. There was a fierce ethnic and religious hatred between Jews and Samaritans in Jesus' day. Jews looked down their noses at the morals and customs of the Samaritans. They were treated the same way as Mexicans are in California. Jesus' story cuts through the convenient way we all have of dividing others into "neighbors" and "enemies."

Love Your Enemies
(Matthew 5:38-48; Luke 6:27-36)

The love-in-action illustrated in Jesus' story of the Good Samaritan was really the trademark of his teaching. He said more about how it turns enemies into neighbors in the collection of teachings called the Sermon on the Mount.

> You have heard that it was said, "You shall love your neighbor and hate your enemy." But I say to you, "Love your enemies."
>
> Matthew 5:43, 44.

These words of Jesus are among the hardest words in the Bible to deal with. Many books have been written in an effort to explain them away.

It's not that we can't understand these words, but rather that we have trouble making them fit with the way things are, especially in wartime. They are as difficult in times of "cold war," when threatening words fly back and forth and defense spending increases, as in times of actual combat between nations.

Jesus is saying that the principle of "loving your own group and hating the hostile outsider" simply will not do. The end result of what Jesus says is that there *are* no more enemies. If we treat a person or a group of persons as neighbors, they can no longer remain our enemies. And if they're no longer our enemies, there's

no reason to hate them. The cycle of hate is broken—
from our end.

Show Some Family Resemblance
(Matthew 5:45-48; 5:9)

Jesus didn't say, "Act this way because I'm telling you
to." He gave a reason.

The reason to love your enemies, says Jesus, is because that's what God does.

For instance, God makes the sun rise on good people
and bad people alike; he sends the rain on those who
are just and those who are unjust. God isn't partial
about where the sun shines and the rain falls. He
doesn't look at people in Ontario or Kansas or Oregon
and decide whether or not they're obeying him before
he makes the crops grow.

"Do you get this point?" asks Jesus. "Do you see that
God doesn't classify people into friends and enemies?
Do you see that he's kind even to selfish, ungrateful
people?

"Well, then, show some family resemblance to God! If
you're sons and daughters of God, then act like it!
Imitate the way he acts. Behave the way he does toward
enemies. If God doesn't divide people into neighbors
and enemies, you shouldn't either!"

In the seventh Beatitude (Matthew 5:9), Jesus says
the same thing: "You're a peacemaker? Well, good for
you! You're showing that you're a child of God; you've
taken on his character."

The Case of the Iranian Hostages

In January 1981, the newspapers and TV networks
were obsessed with 52 American hostages who had just
been freed after spending 444 days in Iranian prisons.

Former United States President Carter flew to West
Germany to greet them just one day after leaving office.

Huge crowds waited for the busload of hostages to arrive in West Point, N.Y. The fanfare included a ticker tape parade in New York City, a reception with President Reagan, a national day of celebration, hometown parades, media interviews, and book contracts. The song, "Tie a Yellow Ribbon Round the Old Oak Tree," was heard everywhere. Yellow ribbons were displayed prominently.

Canadians were caught up in the event too. Ken Taylor, the Canadian ambassador to Iran, and his wife had sheltered six American diplomats and spirited them out of the country; the Taylors were heroes too.

In the middle of all this celebration, a Canadian peace researcher named Ernie Regehr asked a difficult question. Of course we care about the American hostages. Of course we celebrate with yellow ribbons. But if we care about the 52 American hostages and *not* about the 100,000 Iranians who were imprisoned under the Shah, are we not showing "selective compassion"?

Or—to put it another way—if we pay more attention to 52 American hostages than to the fact that *at least* 52 Indo-Chinese boat people died *every day* during those 444 days, are we not showing "selective compassion"?

"Selective compassion" is what Jesus is talking *against* in the Sermon on the Mount. "God doesn't play favorites with his compassion," says Jesus, "so don't you either!"

Earl Martin and the Unexploded Shells

Near the end of the Vietnam War, Earl and Pat Martin lived with their family in Quang Ngai, a town in a northern province of South Vietnam. It was an agricultural area which had seen heavy fighting. The locals were afraid to start working the rice fields again because of all the undetonated explosives buried there. If an unexploded shell hit against a metal plow, the farmer working the land could be killed instantly.

Earl and Pat worked for an American-based church agency. It was Earl's job to find unexploded mines and take them apart and to train the locals to do it also. He decided that it was necessary to do this himself as an American since it was Americans who had put the mines there in the first place.

When people in America asked whether Earl—the father of a young daughter—should really be doing such dangerous work, he replied:

> It's precisely because we do love our daughter that we feel it important to work at cleaning up the countryside. We are mother and father not only to Lara but to all children. . . . No person's life is more or less dispensable than another person's.

Earl also decided that he couldn't allow his compassion towards the Vietnamese farmers to be selective. He had to continue the work whether it was the South or the North who officially controlled the territory. So when the Americans left South Vietnam in the spring of 1975, Pat and the children went too—but Earl stayed. He stayed until the North Vietnamese themselves forced him to leave.

PONTIUS' PUDDLE

I BELIEVE THAT WE CREATURES SHOULD ACT AS GOD'S AMBASSADORS IN THIS SINFUL WORLD.

The Place Where Goodness Happened

During World War II, a French pacifist named André Trocmé served as pastor in the small town of Le Chambon, tucked away in the mountains of southern France. There, under the nose of the occupation government—and with a Nazi SS unit stationed nearby—goodness happened.

It all started when André's wife Magda found a Jewish woman knocking on her kitchen door one night, asking for refuge. "Naturally, come in, and come in," said Magda.

More and more Jewish refugees came to the village, and the "kitchen resistance" picked up momentum. Special homes were set up to receive the guests. Ordinary Le Chambon villagers risked their lives by sheltering and feeding thousands of Jews.

When the Gestapo raided the village looking for Jews, the citizens invited the officers in for a cup of tea. But nobody squealed.

When a researcher came by years later to ask the villagers why they had engaged in this dangerous work, one woman said: "Look, look. Who else would have taken care of them if we didn't? They needed our help, and they needed it *then*."

André Trocmé's favorite Bible passages were said to be the story of the Good Samaritan and the Sermon on the Mount. The villagers understood him when he preached: "There must be no limit to your goodness, as your heavenly Father's goodness knows no bounds." "Be compassionate as your Father is compassionate" (Matthew 5:48; Luke 6:36, NEB).

Are Pacifists Cowards?
(Matthew 5:39-41)

You may have heard of the term "nonresistance." It comes from the King James and Revised Standard versions of Matthew 5:39, which read: "Resist not evil" (KJV) and "Do not resist one who is evil" (RSV).

Often pacifists are thought of as cowards, or as people who lie down and do nothing while evil walks all over them. At first glance, the term "nonresistance" seems to imply that. It sounds like being passive or negative to evil. It also seems to contradict the active peacemaking carried out by people like Earl Martin and the villagers of Le Chambon.

But let's look more closely at what the Bible says. Right after Jesus makes that statement about "nonresistance," he goes on to talk about turning the other cheek and walking the second mile:

> If any one strikes you on the right cheek, turn to him the other also; and if any one would sue you and take your coat, let him have your cloak as well; and if any one forces you to go one mile, go with him two miles.

Turning the other cheek or walking the second mile is a far cry from doing nothing. In Jesus' day it was the hated Roman occupation troops who forced ordinary people to "go a mile" with them as carriers of their supplies.

Jesus is really saying something like this: "Don't

place yourself against an opponent in the normally accepted way (as in 'an eye for an eye and a tooth for a tooth'). Don't respond by treating the person as an enemy. Don't fall into the trap of trying to resist evil with evil methods. Instead, show love-in-action toward the person. Think of your enemy as your neighbor."

When you respond to an opponent in an unexpected way, he or she has to stop for a minute and think how to react. In that moment, she has a chance to hear another voice from within—the voice of God. You don't know whether she will obey that voice, but you have provided the opportunity for it to be heard. That is the important thing.

How William Rotch Resisted the Privateers

During the summer of 1778, a British battleship dropped anchor in the harbor of Nantucket Island, off the New England coast. William Rotch, a leader of the Quaker community on the island, knew that the ship's purpose was to plunder the town.

With the consent of his fellow citizens, Rotch formed a one-man welcoming committee, and greeted Sir Conway-Etherege, the British commander, at the pier. He invited Conway-Etherege home to dinner.

After a pleasant meal, the commander decided to get on with his business. "We're here to plunder," he told Rotch. "As you can see, your little hamlet is completely at our mercy. Where shall we start?"

"I don't know of a better place than here at my house," said Rotch. "I'm better able to bear the loss than anyone else. We have some silver plate, some good, serviceable blankets, and food supplies in the cellar."

Conway-Etherege didn't know what to do. He had never come across this response before! "Tell me," he said, "are there any more men like you on Nantucket?"

"Oh, yes, many better men," said Rotch.

"Well, I want to meet them," Conway-Etherege answered.

So Rotch took him around to meet a shopkeeper who had given 400 barrels of flour to the poor the winter before, and another one who had given away blankets and shoes.

"Would you like to meet more of our people?" asked Rotch.

"Oh, no," replied Conway-Etherege. "I can hardly believe there are three such men as you in the world. A whole street full of them would be too much."

So Conway-Etherege went back to his ship, and Nantucket was saved.

On Enemy Love—Three Objections

As we said earlier, Jesus' statements about enemy love are hard for all of us to deal with. Some of the questions people ask about the Sermon on the Mount are valid—so valid that most of the rest of this book will deal with answering them (in some way or other). Before we go on, here are the three most common objections to taking Jesus' words at face value:

(1) Jesus meant his teaching to apply to our personal enemies, but not to our country's enemies. It

doesn't apply when we're acting as citizens to help defend our society. Jesus, after all, came to save our souls; he had nothing to do with the political affairs of his day.

(2) This teaching is impossible to follow, and God wouldn't ask us to do the impossible. Nobody can show love-in-action even to *neighbors* all the time, let alone to *enemies.* So this teaching must be here in the Bible to let us know every day how much we need God's forgiveness.

(3) This teaching is for some future time, when evil is more under control. Given the evil nature of the world today, it's necessary to use a lesser evil to combat a greater evil sometimes. Things just aren't as black and white as we'd like them to be.

Keep these three objections in the back of your mind. Start thinking about how *you* would answer them.

Review and Reflect
1. Redo the story of the Good Samaritan to take account of ethnic tensions where you live. Make the Good Samaritan a French Canadian in Alberta, a Metis in Winnipeg, a Cuban refugee in Pennsylvania, a Russian diplomat in Washington, a black American in Mississippi. How much

do you think ethnic and class tensions between and within nations have to do with causing wars?

2. Do you believe there are "two ways to destroy an enemy"?

3. Does the arms race, in your view, make us more or less suspicious of "outsiders"?

4. Evaluate the term "selective compassion." Is it possible to be equally compassionate to everybody? If not, what do we do about it?

5. How do you think Jesus interpreted "You shall not kill"? (Bear in mind that the motivation behind murder and war are the same, and that Jesus' teaching made enemies into neighbors.)

6. Does the Sermon on the Mount imply that God has no enemies? What sense do you make of that? (See chapters 3-4.)

Books for (Very) Serious Study

Furnish, Victor Paul. *The Love Command in the New Testament.* Nashville: Abingdon Press, 1972. Chapter 1.

McSorley, Richard. *New Testament Basis of Peacemaking.* Washington: Center for Peace Studies, 1979. Chapter 1.

Piper, John. *Love your Enemies.* Cambridge: Cambridge University Press, 1979. (Warning: this one is a very heavy—but excellent—New Testament study.)

Yoder, John H. *The Original Revolution.* Scottdale: Herald Press, 1971. Chapter 2.

3
What Jesus Did About Enemies

The devil took him to a very high mountain, and showed
him all the kingdoms of the world and the glory of them; and
he said to him, "All these I will give you, if you will fall down
and worship me." Then Jesus said to him, "Begone, Satan!"
—*Matthew.*

We all know that talk can be cheap. Jesus didn't just
stand up in front of a TV camera or a classroom and talk
about peace, however, and then go merrily on his way.

What Jesus *said* fit with what he *did.* In other words,
he validated his preaching with his lifestyle.

Jesus Sweats Out His Career Choice
(Matthew 4:1-11; 3:13-17)

The first glimpse we have of Jesus as an adult, he's in
the desert sweating out his career choice.

"Run that by me again," you may say. "I thought he
was being tempted by the devil!"

Well, he was. But he was being tempted about how to
work out his vocation.

Jesus had just been baptized, that is, he had been
commissioned for a life of service to God. The Spirit had
come upon him (as a dove, not as a hawk or an eagle),
and a voice had said, "This is my beloved Son; I'm

pleased with him. I put my stamp of approval on him."

Jesus was commissioned for a special task. We know now that this task was to be the Messiah. But Jesus had to figure out *how* to be the Messiah.

He had to figure it out not in a vacuum, but in a very specific cultural and political situation. We don't figure out *our* careers in limbo either, but rather in light of what's going on in our country and among our peers at the time—and in light of what people expect of us. For Jesus it was the same way.

Jesus' people, the Jews in Palestine, were under Roman occupation. They expected their Messiah to be a political deliverer. And Jesus had a lot of competition. He wasn't the only person around who was thought to be the Messiah. So it was very difficult for him to come up with the right job description.

The Options Jesus Didn't Take

As Jesus struggled with his career choice out there in the desert, he naturally thought about the political-religious groups that were part of his world. Perhaps he could work out a job description by joining one of them.

He thought about the Pharisees, those traveling teachers who emphasized obedience to the Law. They believed that if only people would obey the Law perfectly, the Messiah would come.

He thought about the Sadducees, those establishment types who ran the temple in Jerusalem. They collaborated a little too much with the Romans to suit many people.

He thought about the Essenes, those monks who lived in caves out in the desert. Their way was one of peace and obedience. But they tried to be faithful by living in their own separated little communities.

Finally, Jesus thought about the Jewish freedom fighters known as the Zealots, whose program included acts of terrorism. During his childhood, he had heard stories about a Zealot named Judas the Galilean.

Judas had been so upset with the Roman census of the Jewish population in 6 A.D.—a census taken for taxation purposes—that he and his followers raided a Roman armaments depot just three miles from Nazareth. The Romans had rewarded them with the usual punishment for political offenses—crucifixion.

Out there in the desert, Jesus thought about his people's continued oppression under Roman rule. He thought, for instance, about the Jewish "tenants" who worked Herod's personal estates. He wondered whether the violent way of the Zealots might be the only way. People expected their Messiah to end Roman rule, after all, and how else could it be done?

But by the time he left the desert, Jesus had refused the option of being the kind of Messiah who conquers with military might—either of the establishment kind or the Zealot kind. He had found another job description.

When the devil showed Jesus all the kingdoms of the world—and offered them to him if only he would use the devil's methods—Jesus said, "Begone, Satan!"

"Okay," said Satan, "but just you wait. I'll be back."

Jesus Confuses Everybody
(Luke 4:18; 7:1-10; Matthew 10:1-4;
Luke 6:12-16; 13:18-21)

Jesus revealed his job description in his own hometown, Nazareth. My job, he said, is to

> proclaim release to the captives and recovering of sight to the blind, to set at liberty those who are oppressed.

Everybody who heard this recognized it as a statement from the prophet Isaiah of what the work of the Messiah was supposed to be.

But when Jesus actually started working, people thought his program was pretty strange. He ate with outcasts—and also with Pharisees. He forgave lower-class folk—and also healed the children of wealthy people. His compassion was definitely not selective. He tampered with the neat categories people had been placed into.

He was so much in tune with God that he was once heard to call God "Daddy." Because of being so in tune with God, Jesus could accurately reveal God's character and show God's nondiscriminatory love.

Jesus taught and demonstrated that even the hated Roman oppressors were not to be considered enemies. He astonished people by healing the servant of a Roman centurion, the commander of a company of 100 soldiers who had the job of keeping the "natives" in line. (When Jesus did this, he commended the centurion's extraordinary faith—and said nothing at all about his profession.) Jesus' action would be like a French doctor healing a Nazi officer during World War II.

Even more astonishing was the unlikely combination of people Jesus chose to be his disciples. One of them—Matthew—was a tax collector. And tax collectors were the worst Roman collaborators you could imagine.

Yet Jesus *also* picked "Simon who was called the Zealot" as a disciple.

With both a Zealot and a tax collector among his followers, how could Jesus carry out any sort of program at all? The disciples themselves couldn't understand it!

But Jesus announced that something exciting was starting to happen right now, and that it would grow like a mustard seed grows into a big tree, or like yeast spreads throughout a whole loaf of bread. The New Testament calls this "exciting something" the kingdom (or reign) of God.

Many people flocked to Jesus. But others were confused—or even threatened. So when the reactions to Jesus started coming in, they weren't all favorable.

I Bring a Sword
(Matthew 10:34-39; Luke 12:51-53; 14:26-27)

At one point Jesus said, "You think I came to give everybody a nice peaceful life? Well, I hate to disillusion you. But you can see for yourselves that the heat's on. I bring a sword. That is to say, my teaching and life are so radical that to follow me can be a dangerous business.

"If you take me seriously, it might even tear some

families apart. They'll be torn right in two, as if a sword plunged into their heart and divided them.

"In fact, if you put your love for your family above your love for me, you're not worthy of me. And if you don't take up your cross and follow me, you're not worthy of me. Anybody who tries to save his life will lose it, and anybody who loses it for my sake will find it."

Now this business about the cross and losing one's life really upset Jesus' followers. For one thing, it was certainly an upside-down way to understand things. It went against all logic.

But it upset the disciples for another reason, too. They had been around. They knew about the fate of Judas the Galilean and his cronies. When Jesus mentioned a cross, they remembered all those political criminals who had died on crosses. But how could Jesus or his followers die as political criminals, when they weren't using the violent techniques of the Zealots? It was all very confusing.

Behold your King—Riding in a VW
(Matthew 21:1-9; Zechariah 9:9, 10)

On the day we remember as Palm Sunday, it finally looked like Jesus was going to be the Messiah people were expecting. Pilgrims in Jerusalem for the Passover festival hailed him as he entered the city.

But something was drastically wrong! To be a proper Messiah, Jesus should be riding a warhorse. Instead, he came on a donkey. It's as if the President of the United States would triumphantly enter Washington today—in an old, battered-up VW beetle.

But then, people remembered. They remembered what the Old Testament prophet Zechariah had said:

> Shout with gladness, daughter of Jerusalem!
> See now, your king comes to you;

he is victorious, he is triumphant,
humble and riding on a donkey,. . .
the bow of war will be banished.
He will proclaim peace for the nations. (JB)

Jesus and the Whip of Cords
(Matthew 21:10-13; Mark 11:15-19;
Luke 19:45-48; John 2:13-22)

Once in Jerusalem, Jesus saw something he really couldn't stomach. The Sadducees who ran the temple were promoting the sale of pigeons, sheep, and oxen in the temple court. Yet this court was to be reserved as a place for "outsiders" (non-Jews) to worship.

Also, Jewish pilgrims were being ripped off. They had to buy "approved" animals for their sacrifices in the temple. And these "approved" animals could only be bought here—in special temple currency and at exorbitant exchange rates.

Jesus surveyed the madhouse and said, "This is supposed to be a house of prayer for everybody! But you've made it into a den of robbers!"

What happened next is a problem for some pacifists. "If Jesus used violence against people even once—for a good purpose—then we can too," the argument goes. "Because Jesus 'cleansed' the temple, we can go to war to bring about justice."

Let's take a closer look at what the Gospel writers tell us about this event, and what they don't tell us.

Matthew, Mark, and Luke tell us that Jesus "drove out" the moneychangers and pigeon sellers; they don't say how. Matthew and Mark add that he overturned their tables. So far, we have Jesus intervening in an active way, and the money changers leaving.

The sticky part comes when we look at John 2, where it says that Jesus made a "whip of cords." The controversy comes in trying to figure out how the whip might have been used.

The RSV Bible implies that Jesus might have hit (or at least threatened) people with it, although it doesn't say so directly:

> And making a whip of cords, he drove *them all*, with the sheep and oxen, out of the temple.

But *Today's English Version* gives a different impression:

> He made a whip from cords and drove *all the animals* out of the Temple, *both* the sheep and the cattle.

Actually, there's a good reason for this difference between translations. The verse in the Greek New Testament is unclear about whether the whip was used on animals or on people. And all our English versions of the Bible are based on the Greek.

So we're really not going to solve our problem by comparing translations. Instead, we need to step back from the story, and see what the Gospel writers want to convey to us through it.

Physical vs. Moral Force

Jesus' authority did not come from a whip of cords. The writers are not describing a battle of *physical* force. (Read the story in any of the Gospels, and see what you think.)

If this had been a battle of *physical* force, the merchants and money changers—not to mention the temple police—could and would have overpowered Jesus. Or, if things had gotten too far out of hand, the soldiers in the nearby Roman garrison would have been pressed into service. They could easily have subdued one lone man with a whip of cords.

But none of that happened because this was a battle of *moral* force. Jesus' authority came from who he was.

There are really only two things you can do with a

person whose power comes from his *moral* force:

(1) You can try to keep him away from the people. That's what President Marcos of the Philippines tried with Pope John Paul in 1981. And with good reason. When the Pope got a chance to speak, he told the peasants that the land belongs to everyone, not just to landowners who raise bananas and pineapples for multinational corporations.

(2) Or, you can kill a person whose power comes from his moral force. That's what happened to Martin Luther King, Jr., in 1968.

But we're getting ahead of our story. There's one more vignette from the life of Jesus we need to look at yet. It's in the Garden of Gethsemane, and I've called it—

Satan's Last Try
(Matthew 26:36-56; Luke 22:40-53)

Remember way back there in the desert, when Satan said to Jesus, "You just wait—I'll come back"? Well, he came back.

In the Garden of Gethsemane, Jesus was sweating it out again. He was sweating and praying so hard it was like big drops of blood falling on the ground. He read the signs as well as anybody else; he knew the end was near.

Jesus didn't want to die; but realistically, were there any other options? Maybe he could still slip out of town and retreat to the desert. Or maybe he could finally act like the Zealot terrorist some people still expected him to be.

The test came soon enough, right after Judas betrayed Jesus to the authorities with the notorious kiss.

The people with Jesus panicked. They fumbled around until somebody found a sword and lopped off the ear of the high priest's servant.

Then Jesus went on a real tirade. "Stop this nonsense!" he said. "Do you mean to tell me that you still don't understand? Don't you realize what power I have at my disposal? Who needs your sword? I could call up 10,000 angels, if *power* was what this is about.

"Once and for all, stop trying to act like Zealot terrorists. Put that sword away! Don't you understand that everybody who takes the sword will die by the sword? That's not the way to protect yourselves. That's not the way to stop the violence of the world. That's not the way to correct injustice.

"Where have you people been for three years, anyway?"

Can Two Swords Be Enough?
(Luke 22:35-38; Matthew 10:1-10; Luke 10:4)

There in the Garden, after Jesus said all this, the disciples thought back to an incident that had happened just hours before. Jesus had been trying to get across to them that some difficult times were ahead.

"Earlier," said Jesus, "a year ago or more, I told you to go out and just take your chances with people. 'Don't take money or sandals or a staff to help you walk or a sword to ward off wild animals and bandits,' I said. 'You'll find people who will take care of you.' You remember that?"

Yes, the disciples remembered.

"But now," said Jesus, "things are going to get pretty hot. You'd better take a purse and bag, and a sword. Be prepared for the worst."

"Oh, look here!" said the disciples. "Here are two swords."

"Enough, enough!" said Jesus, with a wave of his hand. The disciples wondered what he could possibly mean. "Enough for what? What could two swords possibly be enough for?"

Now, after this tirade in the Garden, it was clear what Jesus didn't mean. He didn't mean that his followers should use swords to defend themselves or their op-pressed countrymen or even Jesus himself.

What he did mean was more like, "Enough of this talk! They don't understand what I'm getting at anyway!"

The End Is Just the Beginning

We all know how this part of the story ends. Jesus gets killed—on a cross, like a political criminal. The people say, "Give us Barabbas the Zealot instead. He's the one who can do something for us. We reject Jesus' approach."

Jesus does not resist. In fact, the Gospel writers give the distinct impression that he's letting himself get killed.

But what happened in Jesus' death was far more than anybody could have imagined.

This life, which seemed to the shocked disciples to end in total failure, was God's way of bringing about peace between God and humanity and between persons and groups. It was God's way of undoing the Fall, of re-storing the possibility for harmony which we examined in chapter 1.

The other Messiahs of the first century—Judas the Galilean and all the rest—we've never heard of. Jesus is our Lord and Savior.

By Jesus' resurrection and his aliveness in the church today, God shows us that the way of Jesus is his way. Jesus revealed God's true character. But Jesus also revealed what it's like to be a complete human being. So Jesus' way is to be our way too.

But more of that in the next chapter.

Review and Reflect
1. This chapter highlights the following: (1) how Jesus strug-gled with the question of violence, (2) the problems his dis-

ciples had understanding him, and (3) the nonviolent, non-discriminatory way he related to others. It includes many of the "prooftexts" used by pacifists, and provides a way of understanding some of the texts commonly used *against* pacifists. Look up the references! Where do you agree—or disagree—with the approach of this chapter?

2. What would Jesus have said or done about the Russians? About Latin American military dictatorships? About Third World peasants who grow bananas or sugar for North American consumption? What *wouldn't* he have said or done?

3. Has following Jesus ever brought "a sword" for you? For anybody you know?

4. A church leader from 200 A.D. named Tertullian said this:

How shall the Christian wage war, no, how shall he even be a soldier in peacetime, without the sword which the Lord has taken away [in the Garden of Gethsemane]? . . . Although even a centurion had believed, the Lord afterwards in disarming Peter ungirded every soldier.

What do you think?

Books for (Very) Serious Study

Ferguson, John. *The Politics of Love.* Nyack: Fellowship of Reconciliation, 1977.

Hengel, Martin. *Victory over Violence.* Philadelphia: Fortress Press, 1977.

Sider, Ronald J. *Christ and Violence.* Scottdale: Herald Press, 1979.

Yoder, John H. *The Politics of Jesus.* Grand Rapids: Eerdmans, 1972. Chapter 2.

4
Joining the Army That Sheds No Blood

For he [Christ] is our peace, who has made us both one, and has broken down the dividing wall of hostility.
                                          —Paul.

Christ with his blood gathers the army that sheds no blood.
                              —Clement of Alexandria.

In the last two chapters, we've seen what Jesus said and did about enemies during his lifetime.

Jesus said, "Love your enemies." As a human being like us, he loved people indiscriminately. He loved his enemies to death—his own death, that is.

But we also saw that in Jesus' death far more was happening than anybody could have imagined.

What Really Got Killed on the Cross

For one thing, Jesus' death showed that there *are* no more enemies. "What? Do you really mean that?" you may ask.

Yes. What *really* got killed on the cross is the hostility between God and humanity and between categories of people within humanity. Jesus took all the hostility that divides us, and stopped it by absorbing it in his own person.

57

The paragraph you just read is one of the most important ones in this whole book. It has many implications. They take a while to sink in. The New Testament explores this concept from several different angles. So we need to also.

Stopping the Process
(1 Corinthians 2:7, 8)
In a strange verse in 1 Corinthians, Paul says:

> The wisdom I proclaim is God's secret wisdom, which is hidden from mankind. . . . None of the rulers of this world knew this wisdom. If they had known it, they would not have crucified the Lord of glory (TEV).

This "secret wisdom" is the power of Jesus' death, which absorbed the hostility of the world. God's way of dealing with evil was to stop it by refusing to respond in kind (just like William Rotch in Nantucket stopped the privateers by refusing to respond in kind).

Someone has said, "Everytime it [evil] can get someone to strike back we have a victory for evil. It [evil] feeds upon itself." Jesus stopped the process. He let evil die of starvation.

The Greatest Wall Smasher of Them All
(Ephesians 2:11-22)
A famous poem by Carl Sandburg in *The Family of Man* begins like this:

> There is only one man in the world and
> his name is All Men.
>
> There is only one woman in the world and
> her name is All Women.
>
> There is only one child in the world and
> the child's name is All Children.

God started things out with only one family. Adam, Eve, Cain, and Abel held the promise of all humanity living in harmony.

God's first attempt misfired. A wall of hostility went up—first between God and humanity and then between people. Adam and Eve were kicked out of the Garden. People started assuming they had no responsibility for their brothers and sisters. Cain could coldly murder, and then ask, "Am I my brother's keeper?"

This eventually led to attempts at security like the Great Wall of China—and to walls of missiles aimed at each other by great powers like the United States and the Soviet Union.

But God tried again—with Jesus. That's why the Bible sometimes calls Jesus the second (or last) Adam. As Christians, we are part of God's second try.

Or, to put it another way, Jesus is the greatest wall smasher of them all. He brings back the possibility of people living in harmony—with God and with each other. And we are part of his wall-smashing movement.

A Catholic pacifist named Richard McSorley believes that:

> Peace is always 3-sided—God,
>   self, and neighbor.
> Peace can never leave God out;
>   nor can there be any
> peace with God and myself if I leave
>   my neighbor out.

When Paul works out the implications of this wall-smashing in the book of Ephesians, he sounds downright ecstatic. The greatest division between peoples in his day was the one between Jews and non-Jews. But because of what happened in Christ, says Paul, Jews and Gentiles are no longer enemies. In fact, they are both part of the church!

A Jolt for Poor Peter—and Cornelius Too
(Acts 10)

A case study of this wall-smashing comes when Peter is sent to preach to Cornelius, a Roman centurion. At first Peter is revolted by this idea. After all, he's always been taught to think of Gentiles as "unclean." Besides all this, Cornelius is a career officer in the Roman army (like the centurion whose slave Jesus healed).

But finally Peter obeys and preaches to Cornelius the "way of peace." What a jolt for poor Cornelius! It's like somebody coming up to the commander of a United Nations peacekeeping force and saying, "Hey, I'm going to show you the *real* basis for the way of peace."

We're not told whether Cornelius leaves his police-like peacekeeping profession or stays with it. The story in the book of Acts is not told from Cornelius' point of view, but from Peter's. The incident forces Peter to change some of his prejudices. "I see now how true it is that God has no favorites," he says.

Updating Peter and Paul

Clarence Jordan, working to form an integrated Christian community in Georgia in the 1960's, updated Peter and Paul's insight like this:

"So then, always remember that previously you Negroes ... were at one time outside the Christian fellowship, denied your rights as fellow believers, and treated as though the gospel didn't apply to you, hopeless and God-forsaken in the eyes of the world.

"However, because of Christ's supreme sacrifice, you who were so segregated are warmly welcomed into the Christian fellowship....

"He himself is our peace; it was he who integrated us. And abolished the segregation patterns which caused so much hostility."

Think about the major divisions between peoples in

the 1980's. How would *you* update Paul and Clarence Jordan?

I Pledge Allegiance

The New Testament often mentions the "new humanity" God is creating. The "new humanity" is a way of describing the Christian church, which we belong to as followers of Jesus.

To belong to the church is to have a kind of allegiance to God's kingdom and to the "oneness" it implies which cuts across national boundaries. It means taking a new pledge of allegiance, which might go something like this:

> I pledge allegiance
>   to the cross
>   of Jesus Christ,
> And to the forgiveness
>   for which it stands,
> One church under God,
>   indivisible,
> With liberty and
>   justice for all.

We don't often think about the fact that the church of Jesus Christ has existed under every possible kind of political system (including communism), and that Christians can be found in virtually all countries of the world.

Something dramatic needs to happen—like a pope (John Paul II) being elected from a communist country (Poland), or like a worldwide Christian gathering—before we think about these things.

One worldwide Christian gathering I happen to know is Mennonite World Conference. It was last held in North America in 1978. There in the Wichita Coliseum, people in saris and three-piece suits, Afros and pigtails worshiped God together. The songbook included words in English, French, German, Dutch, Spanish, Russian, Quechua, Cheyenne, Japanese, Portuguese, Tanzanian, Tshiluban, and Somalian.

The Christian church is like popular music or scientific discoveries—national boundaries cannot contain it. The Beatles were popular all over the world. Insulin— a Canadian discovery—is used all over the world. The Christian church is alive all over the world.

The Army That Sheds No Blood
(1 Peter 2:9)

Because the church incorporates all races, the New Testament sometimes refers to Christians as a "new race." "You are a chosen race," says Peter, "a royal priesthood."

Christian writers from the first couple centuries of church history had no trouble making the connection between Christians as a "new race" and nonparticipation in warfare. Our book title comes from Clement of Alexandria (200 A.D.), who said:

> Christ with his blood gathers the army that sheds no blood . . . . We Christians are a peaceful race, bred not for war but for peace.

In July, 1914, just before World War I broke out, a

PONTIUS' PUDDLE

SEE, GOD. WE ALMOST HAVE PEACE IN CENTRAL AMERICA, WE'VE MADE STRIDES TOWARDS ELIMINATING APARTHEID, WE'RE TREATING WOMEN ALMOST LIKE PEOPLE, AND NOW WE'VE SIGNED A TREATY THAT REDUCES OUR NUCLEAR STOCKPILES BY ALMOST TEN % ! PRETTY ENCOURAGING, HUH ?

British Quaker named Henry Hodgkins and a German Lutheran named Friedrich Siegmund-Schultze made the same connection. "We are one in Christ," they said, "and can never be at war." With that statement they shook hands and formed an international peace organization called the Fellowship of Reconciliation, which is still active today.

Our Enemies—Or God's?
(Romans 12:19-21; 2 Corinthians 5:19)

"Of course we don't go to war against our personal enemies," many people say, "but against God's enemies" (like atheistic communists, for instance).

In seventeenth century England, Oliver Cromwell said that the soldier is to "love his enemies as they are his enemies, and hate them as they are God's enemies." Those Puritans who justified exterminating native peoples in colonial New England apparently agreed with Cromwell.

Yet we have seen how Jesus' death means that God has no enemies. Paul says: "Our message is that God was making all mankind his friends through Christ" (2 Corinthians 5:19, TEV).

Christians need to look at unbelievers as potential

followers of Jesus, not as enemies to be killed. As evangelist Myron Augsburger says:

> We cannot take the life of another person for whom Christ died when we are committed to winning that person to the Lord.

But we can also read in the Bible about God's anger against disobedient people. We can find statements about this not only in the Old Testament (which we'll get to in chapter 6), but also in New Testament books like Romans and Revelation.

This is becoming more and more confusing. How are we going to put together God's anger and his love? The fact is that *we* never are going to be able to put them together completely.

What the New Testament tells us, though, is that God's anger is none of our business! It's our business to imitate God's indiscriminate love, not his anger.

Again, Paul says:

> Never try to get revenge; leave that, my friends, to God's anger. As scripture says: Vengeance is mine—I will pay them back, the Lord promises (JB).

(We'd rather say: "Never mind, Lord, I'll do it for you.") Then Paul continues:

> But there is more: If your enemy is hungry, you should give him food, and if he is thirsty, let him drink. Thus you heap red-hot coals on his head. Resist evil and conquer it with good.
> (Romans 12:19-21, JB).

On Enemy Love—Three Objections Revisited

We have spent three whole chapters looking at Jesus. At the end of chapter 2, we listed three objections which people often give to taking Jesus' words on enemy love at face value. Let's go back and see if we're starting to glimpse a way to answer these objections.

Objection Number One
On Public and Private Roles
(1 Peter 2:21; Matthew 25:31-46; Luke 9:23)

According to the first objection, Jesus meant "enemy love" to apply to personal situations only, and not to enemies of our society. Yet we saw in chapters 2 and 3 that with Jesus, it was impossible to separate the "personal" from the "political." His words and actions broke down the hostile categories into which society had placed people. Jesus' program of active, nonviolent love made the authorities nervous—so nervous they killed him.

War is opposed to everything Jesus said, did, and believed in. And the New Testament asks us—over and over again—to follow the way of Jesus. As Peter puts it: "Christ suffered for you, leaving you an example, that you should follow in his steps."

The "problem" of the Christian and war is really very simple, according to the well-known Catholic pacifist Dorothy Day:

> You just need to look at what the gospel asks, and what war does.
>
> The gospel asks that we feed the hungry, give drink to the thirsty, clothe the naked, welcome the homeless, visit the prisoner, and perform the works of mercy. War does all the opposite. It makes my neighbor hungry, thirsty, homeless, a prisoner, and sick.
>
> The gospel asks us to take up our cross. War asks us to lay the cross of suffering on others.

Mark Twain makes the same point in his satirical War Prayer. He imagines a minister standing in front of his congregation, praying for "victory for our side" during wartime. What the minister and congregation are *really* asking, but dare not express out loud, says Twain, goes something like this:

O Lord our Father, our young patriots, idols of our hearts, go forth in battle—be Thou near them!

O Lord our God, help us to tear their soldiers to bloody shreds with our shells.

Help us to lay waste their humble homes with a hurricane of fire; help us to wring the hearts of their unoffending widows with unavailing grief; help us to turn them out roofless with their little children to wander unfriended the wastes of their desolated land in rags and hunger and thirst.

For our sakes who adore Thee, Lord, blast their hopes, blight their lives, water their way with their tears.

We ask it, in the spirit of love, of him who is the Source of Love. Amen.

Objection Number Two
Is God Asking the Impossible?
(Isaiah 2:4; Micah 4:3-4)

According to the second objection, Jesus' teaching on enemy love is not meant to be kept because it's impossible (and God wouldn't ask us to do the impossible).

It *is* true that Jesus' teachings and example are impossible to follow on our own. But Jesus is alive, and with us in the church. His power is available to us through the Holy Spirit. God provides us not only an example, but also a guide.

If we're Christians, it means we've been forgiven by God. And if we're forgiven, we have available the power to forgive others. It's a power that's largely untapped, but it's there.

If we're forgiven, we no longer need to defend ourselves so fiercely to (and from!) God and other people. We don't need to prove that we're better or stronger than other people, because we know God accepts us as we are.

Our self-image no longer demands the most affluent lifestyle and the most sophisticated weapons. It doesn't demand that Middle Eastern oil and South American sugar be *ours.*

Instead of concluding that "God wouldn't ask us to do the impossible," we can be assured that "what God demands, he gives." That is, God enables us to do what he asks of us. Of course we can't do it ourselves.

All this has reminded many Christians of the Old Testament picture of peace involving swords and plowshares (see chapter 1). A second-century Christian named Justin Martyr put it this way:

> We who were filled with war and mutual slaughter and every wickedness have each of us in all the world changed our weapons of war—swords into plows and spears into agricultural instruments.

A sixteenth-century Christian named Menno Simons added:

> The regenerated do not go to war, nor engage in strife. They are the children of peace who have beaten their swords into plowshares and their spears into pruning hooks, and know of no war.

Objection Number Three
Maybe Enemy Love Is for the Future. . . .
(Mark 1:15)

According to the third objection, enemy love is meant for some future time when we can see that God has evil under control.

But the "future time" has already started—with Jesus. He said, "Repent! The reign of God is right here around you now."

In other words, we're living in an era of overlapping time dimensions. (Science fiction writers would call it a timewarp.) In many ways, it's the same old hostile world out there. But in Jesus' life, death, and resurrection,

God's "future time" of peace and harmony had its beginning.

The church—with members from every century, every political system, every continent—is a "sign" of that "future time." When we're living the way of peace, we're living ahead of our time.

It's not that we as Christians refuse to defend our neighbor. It's rather that—because of Christ—we confess that there is no one anywhere who is *not* our neighbor. We already see a glimpse of the new humanity which Jesus came to reestablish.

We already live as if there were peace, and thereby help to bring it about.

Review and Reflect

1. How do *you* put together God's anger and his love?

2. Discuss these ideas from the end of the chapter: (a) when we are living the way of peace, we are living ahead of our time; (b) when we live as if there were peace, we help to bring it about.

3. Do you think the Spirit of Christ would ever lead Christians into war? Why or why not?

4. Analyze the hymns "Soldiers of Christ, Arise" and "Onward Christian Soldiers." How do they relate to the "army that sheds no blood"?

5. Evaluate again the three reasons commonly given for not taking the Sermon on the Mount at face value. What do you think of the statement, "What God demands, he gives"?

6. Imagine for a moment that Jesus is living on earth today. Can you imagine him in army fatigues, sighting down a gun barrel? Can you imagine him throwing a hand grenade or piloting a submarine carrying nuclear weapons? Can you imagine him living in such a way that demands thinking of Middle Eastern oil or South

American sugar as his rightful possession? Relate all this to the fact that Christians are to continue Christ's work on earth.

Books for (Very) Serious Study

Barth, Markus. *The Broken Wall.* Valley Forge: Judson Press, 1970.

Koontz, Ted and Gayle, et. al. *Which Lord?* Scottdale: *Youth Bible Studies,* 1974.

McSorley, Richard. *New Testament Basis of Peacemaking.* Washington: Center for Peace Studies, 1979.

Sider, Ronald. *Christ and Violence.* Scottdale: Herald Press, 1979.

Yoder, John H. *The Politics of Jesus.* Grand Rapids: Eerdmans, 1972. Chapter 11.

Zuercher, Robert. "Suffer as Christ Suffered," "Love as Christ Loved," "Serve as Christ Served," "Forgive as Christ Forgave" in *Youth Bible Studies* (Scottdale, and Newton: Mennonite Publishing House and Faith and Life Press, 1979).

5

Isn't Violence Sometimes the Only Way?

The Lord's my shepherd, says the psalm.
But, just in case, we'd better get a bomb.
　　　　　　　—Tom Lehrer, humorist.

Some Christians throughout the ages have said, "Of course it's true that Jesus defeated evil nonviolently. Ideally, the church should be an 'army that sheds no blood,' with units at the ready all over the world.

"*But* we have to deal with the world as it really is. Sometimes evil is so out of hand that we have to stop it however we can. Take the Russians, for instance; the only thing they understand is a big stick."

And before the Russians, there were the Nazis. And long before the Nazis—way back in the fifth century A.D.—there were the barbarians.

Let's flash back to the fifth century, to the study of a great Christian leader named Augustine.

The Barbarians Are Coming!

Augustine was a bishop in the great North African city of Hippo. He was responsible for the souls of a whole city full of people, and these people were scared. They were scared because the worst was happening—the barbarians were coming.

Christianity had been the official religion of the Roman Empire for almost 100 years now. The people were afraid that if the empire went, so would Christian values. They were not sure the church could preserve these values without the government's help.

Augustine himself wasn't too worried about this. But he knew the "Christian" empire was going to defend itself against the barbarians. And he didn't want his people to stoop to the level of the barbarians. So, sitting there in his study, he came up with a civilized, "Christian" way to conduct wars. It's been known ever since as the "just war theory."

The Just War Theory

First of all, Augustine's theory assumed that one side is completely right and the other side completely wrong. (After all, the barbarians were invading!) Given that, said Augustine, we can wage war as Christians under these conditions:

(1) The war must be properly declared by a legitimate authority. (No sending advisors or troops into Vietnam or Nicaragua without Congress declaring war. No surprise nuclear attacks. No "war by proxy" with arms sales to the side we want to win.)

(2) War must be used only as a last resort, after all other means have failed. (No sidestepping the United Nations.)

(3) The intention of the war must be to restore peace and bring about justice. (Not to preserve our easy access to the cobalt in Zaire or to keep the Russians away from the oil in Iran).

(4) The war must be waged with moderation. The lives of innocent citizens must be protected. The force used must be in keeping with the goal. (No saturation bombing of civilian areas. No nuclear attacks on Hiroshima to show the Japanese we mean business. No

assuming that women and children in remote villages are enemy guerrillas.)

The Barbarians—and Us

Before we go further, it should be said that the barbarians won. In fact, they took over the city of Hippo just as Augustine was dying.

But the odd thing is that despite this catastrophe for "civilization," the Christian church and Christian values *were* preserved. Here *we* are, after all. We're Christians. The Christian church in the twentieth century has members on every continent. We can see now that the Christians of Augustine's time didn't need to be quite so jumpy about the barbarians. God has taken care of things.

But despite this, Christians in great numbers have latched onto Augustine's "just war theory." Great thinkers have tinkered around with it. Until recently, it's been the official position of most Christian denominations which are not pacifist. Like Augustine, these churches have wanted to limit and civilize war.

Yes, But. . . .

But there are several catches. For one thing, the "just war theory" has never *prevented* a war. Nations don't sit down ahead of time and see if a war they intend to wage fits these categories. Instead, the "just war theory" is rather used to justify wars after they've begun.

Secondly, there's something wrong with a theory that lets each country be its own judge when it's already in the middle of a conflict situation. That's like taking at face value what one teenage male says about another teenage male when they're both after the same girl.

A third problem with the "just war theory" is that "if you start a person killing, you can't turn him (or her) off again like an engine." If you have a military establishment programmed to win and a popular mood in the country that requires victory, you can't just turn that off, either. As we saw in chapter 1, lots of people are being paid to "study war." They're not being paid to protect civilians.

Save the Children

George Zabelka was a chaplain with the U.S. Air Force in Japan during World War II. They were "his" boys who dropped the atomic bombs on Hiroshima and Nagasaki. Zabelka knew the United States had a "gimmick bomb" it intended to use on Japan. But he didn't know ahead of time what it was.

Yet he still feels some responsibility for what happened. He feels responsible because he was supposed to be functioning by the "just war theory," which protects civilians in wartime. But even before Hiroshima and Nagasaki, "his boys" were being asked to kill civilians indiscriminately. And he didn't counsel them against it.

Zabelka remembers trying to help a troubled pilot several months before Hiroshima. The pilot was literally going crazy because:

> he had been on a low-level bombing mission, flying right down one of the main streets of the city, when straight ahead of him appeared a little boy, in the middle of the street, looking up at the plane in childlike wonder. The man knew that in a few seconds this child would be burned to death by napalm which had already been released.

The chaplain couldn't help the pilot back then. What was there to say? But he's determined to be more helpful now. Zabelka has become a pacifist, and has dedicated his life to sharing his views with other Christians.

The fact is that our twentieth-century methods of warfare show less and less regard for innocent civilians.

During World War I, five percent of those killed were

civilians. By World War II, it jumped to 48 percent. As many Germans died in the "conventional" saturation bombing of Hamburg as did in the "nuclear" bombing of Hiroshima.

In the Korean and Vietnam wars, the percentage of civilian deaths went up to 85. The "problem" with guerrilla situations like Vietnam or El Salvador is that you can't tell who the "enemy" is. Soldiers in frustration convince themselves that the enemy could be anybody, including women and children in remote villages.

The Next Time Around

The first nuclear bomb killed 100,000 people. Today's nuclear weapons are hundreds of times as powerful as the one released over Hiroshima. Nobody really knows what could happen the next time around. But here are some experts' predictions.

Just one bomb released over Omaha, Nebraska would fill up all the burn treatment centers in the United States. In a major exchange between the United States and the Soviet Union (involving as little as five percent of our stockpiled weapons), the following would happen:

- *In the Northern Hemisphere*—All major cities destroyed. Most people in cities killed by fire and blast. Most people in rural areas killed by radiation.

- *In the Southern Hemisphere*—Millions killed by fallout.

- *Everywhere*—Drastic changes in climate, which would upset patterns of food production. Unknown genetic effects on both people and animals ("killer bees" could be more than just a plot for thriller movies). Disturbances in the earth's ozone layer, which protects us from the sun's rays.

Both the Soviet Union and the United States would

be destroyed as "viable societies," and "nothing we recognize as our free institutions would survive." Radio news, garbage collection, long-distance trucking, city water supplies—all those services we depend on to keep our society functioning would collapse.

Anybody can see that this policy of *M*utually *A*ssured *D*estruction spells MADness. It's MAD because *the solution doesn't fit the problem.* We're prepared to see civilization as we know it destroyed in order to defeat the other guy's system. It's like the sting of a wasp—one moment of sweet satisfaction for the wasp quickly brings about its own death.

You really can't defend a nation against nuclear attack. All you can do is kill off the other side too. Nuclear war is double suicide.

Are Nuclear Weapons a Deterrent?

"Hey, wait a minute!" I can hear some people saying. "You're missing something important. Our country doesn't plan to *use* any of these weapons—at least not first. We just have them as a *deterrent* to keep the other side from attacking *us*."

We need to think through this policy of nuclear deterrence before accepting its "virtues" at face value.

First, many of us would agree that it's immoral to blow up the world with nuclear weapons. Then we need to ask ourselves this question: "Can it be right to *threaten* to do an immoral thing?" (If it's wrong to kidnap, is it okay to threaten to kidnap?) If the answer is *no*, then we cannot justify a policy of deterrence.

Second, if we say, "We'll bomb you if you don't behave," we just might have to do it sometime.

Third, nuclear weapons put us into a spiral of fear which works like this: "The more weapons we build, the less secure we are; therefore we will build more weapons."

Our side was first with Hiroshima, nuclear submarines, antiballistic missiles, cruise missiles, the neutron bomb, and other sophisticated weaponry. The arms race itself makes our block, our street, and our farm a less and less secure place to live.

Fourth, because our world is a sinful place, it's dangerous to have nuclear weapons around. The urge that made Cain kill his brother can now bring an end to the whole business. We're trusting our survival to sinful Cain-type people and to imperfect computers.

Fifth, United States and USSR policy is focusing more and more on weapons with a first-strike capacity. The idea is that "our" missiles might be able to zap theirs before they get a chance to use them.

This new strategy puts our world in a most precarious spot. It is leading some military strategists to fantasize that they could actually *win* a nuclear war. This kind of thinking only means that somebody is more likely to start one. And we've seen that nobody can really predict the results.

What United States President John F. Kennedy said back in the 60s is becoming more and more true: "Mankind must put an end to the arms race or the arms race will put an end to man."

Turning Our Thinking Around

Threatening each other with war is no longer a viable way for nations to settle their differences, as if it ever was. In the present situation, those who belong to the "army that sheds no blood" are not the ones who are crazy.

Leaders can now be found in most Christian denominations who question the "just war theory" as the basis for operating in our world. (For more information on this, see the list of Christian peace organizations at the back of the book.)

What has changed is this. Before Hiroshima, we didn't have the *power* to destroy our world. Now we do. The devil's joke on humanity which we read about in chapter 1 has really gotten out of hand.

Albert Einstein said, "The splitting of the atom has changed everything except our way of thinking." In other words, anybody who thinks we can defeat communism or promote justice in the world by building more or bigger bombs is *simply not thinking straight.* We haven't let ourselves be jolted into the world as it really is. We're still pretending to be back in bow and arrow days.

Well, What Haven't We Tried?

George Orwell, author of the chilling novel, *1984*, has described our situation like this:

It seems doubtful whether civilization can stand another major war, and it is at least thinkable that the way out lies through nonviolence.

Nonviolence is the "technology" that has not yet been explored.

Defending our values by nonviolence doesn't threaten to blow up the world and doesn't dehumanize the enemy. It leaves open the chance that people on different sides of a conflict situation will respond to each other as *people*, rather than as "the enemy."

There are several important historical situations where nonviolence *has* been tried. One example of a people maintaining their values during an enemy invasion came when the Nazis occupied Norway during World War II.

What's a Nice Boy Like You?...

Norwegians, as we all know, are blue-eyed blonds and healthy outdoor types. Adolf Hitler's goal was to build a "pure" Germanic race of people just like them. So when the Nazis invaded Norway, they expected the citizens to be receptive to their view of reality.

But it didn't work out that way. Teachers in elementary and high schools refused to teach ideas found in Nazi-supplied textbooks. About 1300 Norwegians were carted off to concentration camps in the Arctic. After six months, many were sent back to their classrooms. Then they were even more determined not to teach the vile stuff.

A big point with the Nazis was to have pure Germanic types compete in international athletic events. They wanted to show the world that Germanic peoples are better physical specimens than the rest of humanity. So they quickly took over the Norwegian athletic clubs.

But the Norwegians didn't cooperate. Instead, they promptly resigned their memberships. When these Nazi-run clubs tried to put on athletic events, Norwegians neither played nor came to watch.

Also, there was a "state church" in Norway at that time; that is, pastors were employees of the government. After a Nazi official was put in charge of the church, the pastors all resigned their civil service posts. They

stopped accepting salaries, while continuing to work in their congregations anyway.

In the middle of all this, Norwegians were personally friendly rather than hostile to the occupation troops. In other words, they tried to get soldiers to drop their roles by responding to them as *persons.* They tried to make each enemy soldier feel like this:

> What is a nice boy like you doing here? Look at the dirty mess they've got you into, pestering decent folk like your own.

It's true that many Norwegians faced persecution during the Nazi occupation. People were killed. It was not an easy time. But, as evangelist Myron Augsburger puts it:

> We cannot answer the question of war on the basis of whether or not someone must suffer. Of course they will, one way or another. When troops move to take a beachhead, they do so with the conscious plan that they will sacrifice thousands of men.

Many people believe the Norwegian people suffered *less* during World War II than if they had resisted Hitler violently. And Norway was able to preserve its way of life by its policy of nonviolent resistance.

The Case of the Tired Seamstress

Nonviolent methods can also be used to bring about necessary changes within a society. Take, for instance, the case of the tired seamstress.

One day in 1955, a black seamstress named Rosa Parks got tired of standing in the back of the bus when there was room to sit in the middle. So she sat down and was arrested.

Rosa Parks was arrested because after she sat down, the bus filled up with white folks. And the city of Montgomery, Alabama, had a bylaw to take care of that very situation. It said that if whites were standing, blacks had to give up their seats in the middle of the bus. But Rosa Parks kept right on sitting.

When word of her arrest spread, black teenagers started sharpening knives and collecting baseball bats. But black ministers and other community leaders got wind of these violent preparations and called an emergency meeting. They proposed a black boycott of the city buses instead. Among these ministers was Martin Luther King, Jr.

The bus boycott continued for a whole year, until the courts decided that the law must be changed. During that year, the city suffered economic hardship. Nearly 50,000 blacks suffered personal hardship, sometimes walking ten miles a day in addition to doing their tiring work. A few whites started offering black people rides.

The boycott continued with 95 percent cooperation—and no violence by blacks. And Martin Luther King became more and more dedicated to working for change through nonviolence.

One night, a bomb exploded on King's front porch. No one was hurt, but they easily could have been. King's young children were inside the house.

After this incident, King said to the crowd that had gathered:

If you have weapons, take them home; if you do not have them, please do not seek to get them.... We must love our white brothers no matter what they do to us.... Jesus still cries out in words that echo across the centuries: "Love your enemies; bless them that curse you; pray for them that despitefully use you!" This is what we must live by. We must meet hate with love.

The reason for this approach, as Jesus showed, is that love is the only power that can overcome evil.

Nonviolent methods do not add to the amount of destruction in the world. Sure, they are a risky business. But so is war.

Review and Reflect

1. Which method of defense do you think has more chance of preserving our values against the USSR: Mutually Assured Destruction, or civilian defense of the type Norway used? What do you think would happen if the U.S. and Canada used one fourth of their military budgets for training people in nonviolent methods?

2. Can being killed by an atomic bomb serve any useful purpose?

3. How do you think the "just war theory" stacks up in today's world?

4. After World War II, the Japanese wondered: "How can a nation [the United States] that presumes to worship a God of love condone dropping the atomic bomb on Hiroshima?" Your answer?

5. In the 1930's, Mahatma Gandhi led India's nonviolent campaign for independence. Someone has said of it:

The British beat the Indians with batons and rifle butts. The Indians neither cringed nor complained nor retreated. That made England powerless and India invincible.

How do you explain that?

6. What do you think would happen if we began to reduce our

arms before the "other side" does? What will happen if we don't reduce our arms?

Books for (Very) Serious Study

Brown, Robert McAfee. *Making Peace in the Global Village.* Philadelphia: Westminster Press, 1981.

Douglass, James W. *The Non-Violent Cross.* New York: Macmillan, 1966.

Kownacki, Mary Lou, ed. *A Race to Nowhere: An Arms Race Primer for Catholics.* Chicago: Pax Christi, 1981.

McSorley, Richard. *Kill for Peace?* New York: Corpus, 1970.

Miller, William Robert. *Nonviolence: A Christian Interpretation.* New York: Association Press, 1964.

Regehr, Ernie. *Militarism and the World Military Order: A Study Guide for Churches.* New York: World Council of Churches, 1980.

6
What About War in the Old Testament?

Fear not, stand firm, and see the salvation of the Lord, which he will work for you today; for the Egyptians whom you see today, you shall never see again. The Lord will fight for you, and you have only to be still.

—Moses.

"Yes, war is a risky business in our world," I can hear somebody saying. "Yes, Jesus showed us the way of peace. But what about the Old Testament? God's people fought many wars then. God commanded them to hack his enemies to pieces! God even referred to himself as a warrior.

"So, did God change his mind between the Old Testament and Jesus? (If he did, he's wishy-washy.) Or, if he didn't change his mind, then maybe he still commands us to fight wars in our world today.

"If God worked with a special nation—Israel—in the Old Testament, how do we know he's not trying to work with special Christian nations like ours today?"

These are tough questions. To answer them, we'll have to plunge right in and analyze Israel as a fighting nation.

The first point to notice is that bloody battle scenes

are not equally distributed throughout the Old Testament. We mostly read about God "commanding wars" during two phases of Israel's long history: (1) the period of the conquest and the judges, when the Promised Land is being settled (1250-1025 B.C.) and (2) the era when King David and his successor Solomon reigned (1000-925 B.C.)

Israel's history doesn't begin with Joshua's "conquest" of the Promised Land. And the Old Testament doesn't end with Solomon's reign. To properly understand those 325 years between Joshua and Solomon, we must also look at what went on before and after.

The First and Most Important Story
(Exodus 3:1—4:5; 14:13-14; 15:1, 3)

We begin with the most important Bible story in the Old Testament, a story which at first glance doesn't seem to have much to do with war and peace. The name of this very important story is "God Delivers People," and it goes like this:

God sees a group of oppressed slaves in Egypt and decides to show them he is a deliverer. He recruits a reluctant fellow named Moses to cooperate with him in freeing these slaves. He convinces Moses that the only military hardware needed for this effort is what Moses has in his hand—an ordinary shepherd's rod.

The climax of this escape story is the crossing of the Red Sea. The slaves think the chariots of the Egyptian army are overtaking them, so they fly into a panic. "Why did you make us leave Egypt?" they scream at Moses. "It's better to be slaves than to be dead!"

But Moses reassures them:

Fear not, stand firm, and see the salvation of the Lord, which he will work for you today; for the Egyptians whom you see today, you shall never see again. The Lord will fight for you, and you have only to be still.

Moses lifts up his ordinary rod, an east wind changes the course of the sea, and the escaping slaves walk through. But when the Egyptians try to follow, their chariot wheels get caught in the mud, and God changes the sea back to its usual course. And that's the end of the Egyptians!

One of the oldest pieces of poetry in the Bible is a worship song used by the Israelites to celebrate this event:

> I will sing to the Lord, for he has
> triumphed gloriously;
> the horse and his rider he has
> thrown into the sea. . . .
> The Lord is a man of war;
> the Lord is his name.

The Exodus story and worship song present God as a warrior for the first time in the Old Testament. "The Lord will fight for you, and you have only to be still," says Moses. "The Lord is a man of war," says the worship poem.

God is trying to get across the idea that people can trust in him for deliverance. He is in control of the situation, and he intervenes for people in powerful ways.

God Is a Warrior—He Intervenes for Us
(Ephesians 6:10-18)

To say that God is a warrior is like saying he's a father or a shepherd or a rock. We can relate to these images for God because they come from our own experience or from what we see happening around us. They tell us that God is trustworthy, that he has our welfare in mind, that he looks after us.

But images can be carried too far. When we say that God is our Father, for instance, we don't mean that he got together with a female deity to "father" us. We don't even mean that "he" is male. Each image is only a partial picture which helps us to understand something important about God.

To say that "God is a warrior" does not necessarily mean that he approves of war. The New Testament uses "warrior imagery" too. The "whole armor of God" described in Ephesians 6 has nothing to do with Christians killing other people. How could it, when our feet are to be "shod. . . . with the equipment of the gospel of *peace*"?

So then, why do biblical writers use such confusing images as "God is a warrior"? They do it because we understand battles. We see battles of all sorts around us. Battles are a fact of sinful life. The words "God is a warrior" help us to understand that he intervenes for us.

God Uses Plan B

But—oh, dear—we have left the freed Israelite slaves behind. We've gotten them across the Red Sea by God's intervention. Now comes the conquest of the Promised Land.

But the Bible really doesn't give us a clear picture of how this "conquest" took place. The book of Joshua gives the impression of a steamroller effect, while the book of Judges implies that the land was only settled in "pockets" with "defensive raids" rather than "offensive campaigns."

We don't know what would have happened if the escaped slaves had completely understood and accepted that God wanted to be their warrior. The fact is that they didn't relax and let God handle matters in his own way. They decided God must want them to do battle for him.

The Israelites' lack of understanding doesn't make

them dimwits while we're superintelligent. They didn't have Jesus to show them the way. They only had partial "pictures" of God—pictures like warrior, shepherd, and father.

At any rate, the Israelites couldn't quite grasp or trust God's first battle plan—the one in which he would intervene for them. But God didn't give up on his escaped slaves. Instead, Plan B went into effect. The Israelites fought.

But even while they fought, God impressed upon them in various ways that the victory came from *him*—not from their military efforts. When we read certain Old Testament battle accounts, we can hear in them echoes of the same trust in God found at the crossing of the Red Sea.

Bible scholars have a technical name for this type of battle. They call it "Holy War"—or better yet, "Yahweh's War" (since Yahweh is the Hebrew word for God).

Three Wacky Battles

Three of the wackiest battles of all time are written up in the Old Testament. All of them deal with Israel's reliance on God as warrior between 1250 and 1025 B.C. Here is a reading guide to these three battle stories, to help you look for certain things. Take a Bible and read them through for yourself. They're far more exciting than most TV movies.

The Battle of Jericho (Joshua 5:13—6:21). This is the first major "battle" in the Promised Land. Although Joshua seems to be the leader, he's not really the commander of the troops. An angel comes to him and says, "*I* am the captain of the army of the Lord."

Before the battle even starts, God makes a strange announcement: "See, I have given into your hand Jericho, with its king and mighty men of valor." Then he presents the wacky battle plan: march around the city for seven days, play your trumpets, and shout!

The "walls fall down" on schedule. What's left for Joshua's troops is the mop-up operation.

Gideon against the Midianites (Judges 6 and 7). The Israelites are settled in the land now, but the Midianites keep harassing them. These nasty raiders steal Israelite crops and animals, and even force the inhabitants to hide out in caves for safety.

God calls a judge named Gideon to deal with the situation. Gideon at first protests that he's not the right person for the job—his family is small, and he himself is unknown. But finally Gideon agrees, and manages to raise an army of 32,000.

Then God says, "Hey, hold on a minute! That's far too many recruits. If you fight the Midianites with that many troops, you'll convince yourselves that *you're* responsible for the victory. Let's figure out a way to send most of them home!" (Check your Bible to see what these novel schemes were!)

Gideon raids the Midianite camp at night with only 300 troops armed with trumpets and pottery jars. The awful racket of 300 blasting trumpets and 300 shattering jars rouses the Midianites out of a deep sleep. Convinced that the Israelites are attacking with a huge army, the Midianites kill off each other in a mad scramble to escape.

David and Goliath (1 Samuel 17)—Our last wacky battle comes from the time period of Israel's first king, Saul. It's the story we all learned in Sunday school about little David with his slingshot. The stone from the slingshot stuns Goliath and knocks him down, so that David can get close enough to finish the giant off with his sword.

Again, the idea is that in a "battle" won against such odds and with such unorthodox methods, God must be doing the fighting.

Mopping Up the Enemy
(Joshua 6:15-21)

There's one aspect of the Holy War concept which pacifists have a hard time dealing with. In fact, all civilized, modern people find it difficult to stomach. Bible scholars have named it "the ban." We'd just call it "mopping up the enemy."

In the story of the battle of Jericho, "the ban" works like this: Joshua tells the people that "the city and all that is within it shall be devoted to the Lord for destruction." And sure enough, a few verses after the "wall fell down flat," Joshua's troops

> utterly destroyed all in the city, both men and women, young and old, oxen, sheep, and asses, with the edge of the sword.

At various places in the Old Testament, three reasons are given or implied for this practice:

First, if the victory is God's, then the people shouldn't benefit from it in any way. If everybody and everything is destroyed, there can be no "spoils of battle" to tempt the Israelites.

Second, if the defeated enemy is allowed to live, his pagan religion might be a bad influence on the Israelites.

Third, the defeated enemy deserves to be killed, because he is fighting against God and God's people.

Now the first two reasons seem laudable enough in and of themselves, even though we can't stomach the idea of slaughtering people to achieve them. The third reason is itself a real problem, especially when we remember that Jesus' objective was to make *everybody* "God's people." But we'll get back to that.

In the meantime, let's look at another Old Testament story—not for the squeamish—in which the principle of "the ban" is at work.

King Saul, King Agag—and Us
(1 Samuel 15)

When King Saul is fighting the Amalekites, he fudges on the provisions of "the ban." He decides to save King Agag and the best of the sheep and oxen, and to "utterly destroy" only what *he* considers to be "despised and worthless."

In other words, "the ban" was needed because of people like Saul. He's trying to save some of the spoils for himself. And to top it off, he lies about what he's doing.

He goes to Samuel, God's prophet, and says, "Well, I've done what I'm supposed to."

"Oh, yea?" asks Samuel. "Why is it then that I hear sheep bleating and oxen lowing?"

"Oh, well, yes—them," stammers Saul. "We saved them so we could sacrifice them to God. The people insisted on it!"

Samuel sees this "explanation" as the excuse it is. As the story unfolds, he fulfills "the ban" himself by hacking Agag to pieces. And thus the story ends.

It's hard for us to make sense of hacking King Agag to pieces. We could list the reasons behind this type of total mop-up policy, as we did above. We could even go along with certain Bible scholars who wonder whether "the ban" was really meant to be carried out.

We could compare the number of battles in which it was used with the number in which it wasn't. We could compare Israel's battle practices with those of her neighbors. *But none of that takes away the horror of what is on the page in front of us.* We can't easily explain it away—nor should we try. But we can perhaps learn from it.

The ban makes clear to us that war, *especially* Holy War, is not nice. Whether it's hacking King Agag to pieces or sending a cargo of Muslim thumbs back home to the Greek emperor (in the Middle Ages) or leveling whole Vietnamese villages—war is not nice.

In fact, as generals are the first to admit, war is hell. The Old Testament—which is an "adult" book—does not try to hide that fact.

But, if Holy War is hell ("hell" being the result of sin), then we still have a big problem. The Old Testament seems to imply, then, that God is mixed up in our sin— and even that he commands it.

We can get more perspective on this problem by looking at one last Old Testament story. It takes place about 1025 B.C., and provides one explanation why Israel started to be ruled by kings.

The Latest Model in Chariots
(1 Samuel 8)

In this story, the people are clamoring to Samuel, their prophet-judge, for a king. "They want a king?" says God to Samuel. "They don't want to be ruled by judges anymore? Don't *you* take offense, Samuel. It's not you they're rejecting. It's *me*, God! I've tried to show them all along—ever since I delivered them from Egypt—that *I* want to be their king.

PONTIUS' PUDDLE

IF THE GOOD LORD MEANT FOR US TO LOVE EVERYBODY HOWCUM HE CREATED ENEMIES?

"Okay, Samuel, if the people insist on having a king, let's give them one. But first, I want you to warn them about kings.

"Tell them that their king will think he needs so-phisticated equipment—the latest model in chariots. And if he has chariots, he'll need men to drive them and wax them and grease them. He'll also want men to groom and feed and grow grain for the horses which will draw the chariots.

"And, oh, yes, don't let them forget about the men needed to run in front of the chariots to clear people out of the way; and the military strategists and the unit commanders; and the forced labor in the sword fac-tories and the chariot assembly plants. Tell them not to complain to me when their sons are conscripted for all these jobs!"

So Samuel said all this, but the people didn't pay any attention. "We want to be like the other nations!" they replied. "We want a king to go out and fight our battles!"

"Okay," said God. "You asked for it."

Our God Doesn't Give Up

Some Bible scholars give a fancy name—the "per-missive" or "remedial" will of God—to what this story describes. Quite simply, that means *our God doesn't give up on people.* He didn't in Old Testament times, and he doesn't today. If he did, we'd all be out of luck!

Let's imagine for a moment that God is a potter, and he's working with us on a potter's wheel. He's trying to shape us into tall, graceful vases. But we insist on mov-ing a different direction, and end up as short squatty flowerpots. When that happens, God doesn't throw us out in disgust. Instead, he works with what he has—he allows Plan B to go into effect.

War always was, is, and will be sin. God did not and does not "will" sin. However, God can make use of situations tainted with sin. God cares about us enough that he's willing to work with situations as they are.

During the conquest period, the Israelites didn't understand all God meant by being a warrior for them. They chose the security of doing it themselves. With this mindset, they believed it was God's will for them to totally mop up the enemy. Under these circumstances, they "heard" this as a "command" from God.

When this happened, God didn't retreat into heaven in dismay. He stuck with his people.

Then at the time of Samuel, the Israelites decided they wanted a king who would conduct wars like other nations. And God didn't give up on them then, either.

The fact that God was able to "make use of" wars in the Old Testament—that he even "commanded" them as "second best"—is no excuse for us now; Jesus has clearly shown us that enemies are to be loved.

David Isn't the Last Word
(1 Chronicles 22)

David was the one king of Israel who actively engaged in aggressive military campaigns. One of the reasons the Old Testament gives for David not building the temple in Jerusalem is that he had "shed much blood." His son Solomon—who was to be a "man of peace"—built it instead.

It's important to remember that Israel as a "powerful" military nation is not the Old Testament's "last word." It's not as if God "worked through" a powerful military nation all through the Old Testament—until the minute Jesus was born—then suddenly switched gears completely and latched onto the church.

The united kingdom of Saul, David, and Solomon lasted only 100 years, until about 925 B.C. After that, the divided kingdom of Israel in the North and Judah in the South fell on worse and worse times.

Assyria conquered the Northern Kingdom in 722 B.C.; the Southern Kingdom continued, but only as Assyria's vassal. Then in 587 B.C. what was left of Judah fell to the Babylonians, and most of the leaders were carted off into exile. God's people simply didn't exist as a nation anymore.

All during this period, the Old Testament prophets helped the Israelites put this shocking series of events into perspective. They even forced the people to take a second look at the conquest period of their history (just as we in North America have to take a second look at how our ancestors settled the land at the expense of the native peoples.)

Isaiah's Second Look
(Isaiah 10:5-6; 45:1-6; 43:8-13; 42:1-4; 31:1; 53)

Many of the writings which forced Israel to take a "second look" at her history are found in the book of Isaiah. Here are three important conclusions Isaiah tried to impress upon the people:

(1) "You have to broaden your idea, Israel, of what it means to be a chosen people. You have to understand that you're not the only people God can use to bring about his purposes.

"If God can use you in special ways, he can also use those awful Assyrians; he can even call that pagan conqueror Cyrus 'my anointed'—and we always thought that title was reserved for our own kings.

(2) "You have to understand, Israel, that if you are special or chosen, it is so you can show God off to the world. God's long-range plan is for everybody to understand that he is the deliverer.

(3) "Your special mission of showing God off to other nations cannot be accomplished by killing them off! So stop trusting in chariots! Consider an entirely different

way of operating. Consider being a servant.

"In fact, God wants you to be a *suffering servant.* Out of your suffering obedience will come great benefit for others."

That's a summary of some of the poems found in the book of Isaiah. When Jesus read Isaiah more than 500 years later, he took it very seriously. So seriously that he modelled his own career on Isaiah's *suffering servant.*

And Jesus expects us to take Isaiah seriously, too. God's people as a powerful military nation is simply not the last word—not even in the Old Testament.

Review and Reflect
1. Do you think we can use the Old Testament to justify our country (or any other country) going to war today? Why or why not?

2. Have you ever been in a situation where you felt God was "fighting" for you? Does it make you uncomfortable that the Bible calls God a "warrior"?

3. Look up the story of the Red Sea in Exodus 14 and 15, as well as the Bible passages about Jericho, Gideon, and David and Goliath. What features of "trusting in God" can you find in these stories?

4. Think of times when God didn't give up on you, even though what you decided was "second best" and not what God wanted. Does that mean God was "mixed up" in your sin? Relate your experience to the Old Testament.

5. What can we learn from the slaughters that went on under the Old Testament provision called "the ban"?

6. Do you think God "changed his mind" between the time of David and the time of Jesus? If not, what did happen?

Books for (Very) Serious Study
Craigie, Peter C. *The Problem of War in the Old Testament.* Grand Rapids: Eerdmans, 1978.

Eller, Vernard. *War and Peace from Genesis to Revelation.* Scottdale: Herald Press, 1981. Chapters 2-4.

Lind, Millard C. *Yahweh Is a Warrior.* Scottdale: Herald Press, 1980.

Yoder, John H. *The Original Revolution.* Scottdale: Herald Press, 1971. Chapter 4.

7

Aren't We Supposed to Obey the Government?

Our country: in her dealings with foreign nations may she always be in the right; but our country, right or wrong.
　　　　　　　　—Stephen Decatur (War of 1812).

You shall have no other gods before me.
　　　　　　　　—First Commandment.

We've struggled with the Old Testament. We've heard Jesus' invitation to join the army that sheds no blood. We've seen how dangerous violent "solutions" are in our nuclear age.

But sometimes our countries ask us to fight for them—or to support direct preparations for violence against others. We like being American or Canadian. So, shouldn't we show our patriotism and loyalty by obeying their requests?

In case you didn't know, this is one of the hottest topics for Christian discussion. So, welcome to the debate!

The Hottest Debate Around
(Mark 12:17; Romans 13:1, 2)

We all bring two things to this debate, whether we recognize it or not. The first is our own understanding of two passages from the New Testament. Everybody has these two passages rolling around in the back of their minds somewhere.

One is from the Gospels, and goes like this:

> Jesus said to them, "Give back to Caesar what belongs to Caesar—and to God what belongs to God" (JB).

Caesar isn't with us anymore, of course. So nowadays we use the word "Caesar" to symbolize the power of our nation over us.

The second passage in the back of everybody's mind comes from Paul, and begins like this:

> Every person must submit to the supreme authorities. There is no authority but by act of God, and the existing authorities are instituted by him; consequently anyone who rebels against authority is resisting a divine institution (NEB).

The other thing everybody brings to this debate is his or her own personal feelings about government and law. Take a minute to work through the following quiz. Get in touch with how *you* feel about breaking the law—any kind of law.

Keep Off the Grass—A Quiz

Question 1. Are there any categories of "law" you would feel okay about breaking? Think about these:

(a) a city ordinance telling you to Keep Off the Grass;

(b) the speed limit;

(c) your family's curfew "law";

(d) a U.S. or Canadian law requiring you to register for the draft;

(e) a court injunction forbidding people to demonstrate in front of nuclear power plants.

Question 2. How do you decide when (if ever) it is legitimate to break a law? Think about how these factors enter in:

(a) your respect (or lack of it) for those making the law;

(b) the seeming importance of the law;

(c) the seeming "rightness" of the law;

(d) the fear of punishment;

(e) the potential hassle of either keeping or breaking the law.

Store all this for later reference.

The Case of the Competing Circles

Many people have a diagram in their heads on how they think God and Caesar relate to each other in society. The most common diagram puts God and the state side by side as two separate but equal "areas of activity" (or spheres) that call for our loyalty and obedience:

This diagram gets us into trouble at one place. It implies that there's a "grey area" where God and the state conflict with each other:

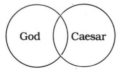

What do we do when God asks for one kind of action (join the army that sheds no blood!) and our country asks the opposite (fight to preserve our interests!)?

Some people say, "Well, in that case we should obey

our country unless the Bible explicitly tells us *not* to do that particular thing." Others say, "No, no! Feel free to disobey the government unless the Bible tells us specifically to *obey* in that case."

The Case of the Superimposed Circles

Grey areas are uncomfortable. So some people avoid them by using a different diagram. This diagram is a little hard to put on paper, but it's as though the circle representing God and the circle representing Caesar were superimposed on each other. In other words, if you move the two circles on top of each other, you've done away with the grey area:

In this diagram, if we obey our government we *are* obeying God. Then what God asks and what Caesar asks are really not contradictory at all. What we do through our government is our way of serving God.

As we saw in the last chapter, this solution has been around since Old Testament times. It's also the assumption many Christians operate under today, often without realizing it.

For instance, it's the assumption behind this statement by a TV evangelist:

> All ablebodied United States male citizens are obligated to fight to the death, if necessary, to defend the flag.

It's also the assumption of a five-year-old friend of mine named Jeanette.

Jeanette and Her Flag

One night when I was visiting at Jeanette's house, she showed me an American flag she had made in kindergarten class.

It was a nice flag for a five-year-old. But when I looked at it more closely, I realized that one of the stripes was pasted on the paper vertically and seemed to form a cross with one of the horizontal stripes.

"What's that?" Jeanette's Daddy asked.

"Don't you know?" she answered, disgusted that anybody should be so stupid. "That's for Jesus, because we're free."

For Jeanette, Jesus and the flag (God and Caesar) are so mixed together that she can hardly think about one without the other.

The Circle as Large as the Universe

But there is still another diagram. It starts with a circle as large as the universe. That circle represents God's rule over the universe. Within that circle, there's another smaller one. That represents the role of governments within God's rule of the universe:

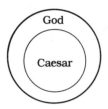

In this diagram, we don't start with the question, "What belongs to Caesar?" but rather with "What belongs to God?" It becomes obvious, then, that *everything* belongs to God. Once that's settled in our minds, we can start working at the question of what belongs to Caesar.

In case you haven't guessed, I find this last diagram the most helpful one in sorting out our obligations in today's world. It's also the one that makes the most sense of Jesus' encounter with the Herodians and the Pharisees.

Tiberius and the Laurel Wreath
(Mark 12:13-17)

Things were getting rough for Jesus. The end was near. One day the Pharisees and the Herodians approached him together with a question. This was very strange, since they were not natural allies. But by now, they both wanted him off the scene.

The question they asked is this: "Tell us, Teacher! Should we pay taxes to Caesar, or shouldn't we? The poll tax, for instance?"

They thought they had Jesus on this one. If he said "No," the Herodians would run off and report him as an anti-Roman agitator. If he said "Yes," the Jewish nationalists would have more ammunition against him.

But Jesus responded quite calmly. "Bring me a denarius," he said. "That's the coin you're supposed to use to pay the poll tax, right? Well, I want to have a look at one."

A ripple went through the crowd. Would Jesus' ques-

tioners dare produce a denarius? Finally somebody handed him a coin.

"Well, now," asked Jesus, "whose picture is this? Whose title is inscribed here?"

"Caesar's," somebody said.

Jesus looked at the coin more closely. Yes, there was a picture of Emperor Tiberius, wearing a laurel wreath. And a laurel wreath was a symbol of divinity. There under the picture was the phrase, "Emperor Tiberius, august Son of the august God."

Jesus' questioners were losing ground fast, and they knew it. Having a coin in your purse that says "Caesar is divine" was pretty close to worshiping another god. And the first commandment of all is quite clear that "you shall have no other gods before me."

Jesus knew what was going through the minds of the crowd. So this was his answer: "You're carrying around a picture of a god? Well then, if you've declared yourself for Caesar, you may as well give back to your god what belongs to him. But remember to give back to the God of the universe what belongs to *him!*"

Jesus' audience looked at him in amazement. They were operating under Diagram 3. They knew that absolutely *everything*—including all our allegiance—belongs to God.

Paul and the Jumpy Roman Christians
(Romans 12:14—13:10)

The Roman Empire had been good to Paul. The Romans weren't the ones who kept throwing him in jail! Their topnotch road system enabled him to go and preach wherever he pleased. The world Paul knew was at peace, with the Roman army serving everyone as a police force.

But the Christians in Rome were more jumpy about the empire. After all, they were in the middle of it all. They weren't exactly being persecuted—that mad emperor Nero wasn't acting up yet. But they did have to be careful about how and where they worshiped.

Paul wasn't sure what the Roman Christians might do. He didn't want them to act like Zealots and try to oppose the empire in some way. So he reminded them that governments *do* have certain functions, and he listed what some of them were.

A government, said Paul, is supposed to organize things in an orderly way so people can live their lives in peace. Also, it's supposed to carry out a police function—to restrain wrongdoers so organized society can go on. In other words, governments have a specific role in God's universe. In that sense, they are God's agents.

Paul *didn't* mean to suggest that any government which happens to be in power is specifically put there by God, or that whatever any government decides to do is God's will. Paul is *not* saying, "There is no Hitler but by act of God, and Hitler is instituted by him." It *is* true that nothing happens which God doesn't permit. But God is not morally responsible for Hitler.

God instituted marriage and God instituted government. But that doesn't make every marriage—or every government—a good one.

It's useful to remember that the same Roman government Paul is writing about in Romans 13 eventually killed him. The anti-Christian rage of Nero caught him, too. Nobody in his right mind would claim that Nero was God's agent—not even Paul.

The Roman Government Revisited
(Revelation 13)

A later New Testament writer gives a totally different picture of the Roman Empire from Paul's. It's hard to believe that Romans 13 and Revelation 13, penned within 40 years of each other by Paul and John, are both written about the same empire.

In Revelation 13, John uses metaphorical language to comment on the Roman emperor Domitian's persecution of Christians. He calls Domitian "the beast." For a time, says John, "the beast" is given the power to "cause those who would not worship the image of the beast to be slain."

Christians in Asia Minor (present-day Turkey) were being arrested in huge numbers. They had one way to save themselves. They could offer a sacrifice in front of an image of Caesar and say, "Caesar is Lord—Jesus be cursed." Those words would save them. Otherwise, they would be executed.

Obviously, these Christians did *not* believe they should "obey Caesar" in this case. They did *not* believe God was working out his will through Caesar, as in Diagram 2. They did not curse Jesus.

Instead, they focused on Diagram 3. They saw Caesar trying to break out of his little circle and take over God's rule of the world. In doing this, Domitian was creating chaos instead of order.

The Parade Marshall and the Circles
(Colossians 2:15)

The case of the Roman government shows that *any* government can (and frequently does) get out of hand.

This isn't surprising, since countries are, in one sense, just a lot of people lumped together.

We saw in chapter 1 how human beings tend to forget about their specific functions and try to take over the whole thing (remember the composer and the orchestra members?). Well, the same thing happens with governments.

Paul sometimes uses metaphorical language to talk about this. He refers to the state—and other organisms which are meant to keep life organized—as the "principalities and powers."

In Colossians, he's just been talking about what Jesus did for us on the cross. Then, in a strange verse, he adds this about the "principalities and powers":

He [Christ] disarmed the principalities and powers and made a public example of them, triumphing over them in him.

Paul is describing a parade—a victory procession, in fact. Jesus' death shows that he's the parade marshall of the universe, says Paul. And Jesus' parade has a place for governments. The principalities and powers are supposed to fall into step behind Jesus in this parade—just like we are. But they're not supposed to try to lead it.

Or, as Diagram 3 puts it, governments have an important role as a small circle within the larger one—just like individual orchestra members have an important role in the symphony.

But often, governments—even our own good governments—don't recognize that they're supposed to have that kind of relationship to God's purposes. So they continue to overstep their God-ordained boundaries just as we individual human beings continue to overstep our own limitations. In the same way, governments continue to try to take over the whole circle, the whole parade, the whole symphony.

Emperor Worship, Mars and Us

Old gods don't die—they just recycle themselves and come back in other forms.

Emperor worship isn't dead. It happens when we allow our countries to take on functions that belong to God. It happens when, during an arms race, we let our countries think of themselves and their values as more important than life itself. It happens when we believe that "this nation serves as the *only barrier* to worldwide communist occupation." (The *only barrier*? Doesn't God have something to do with it too?)

Mars, the Greek god of war, isn't dead either. During wartime—and during an arms race—our countries hand over a lot of power to him. As United States President Woodrow Wilson said:

> If you are determined to be armed to the teeth, you must obey the orders and directions of the only men who can control the great machinery of war.

When we give such absolute power to government, we are bowing down to Mars, a pagan, idolatrous god.

Does Submission Mean Obedience?
(Romans 12:14—13:10)

What do we do when our countries step out of line in the parade and ask us to come along with them? Does "to submit" necessarily mean "to obey"? What Paul said to the Roman Christians can help us out here.

Some people try to read the first seven verses of Romans 13 without paying any attention to what comes right before and after them. But Paul wasn't that disorganized a writer. He didn't just put Romans 13:1-7 down in the middle of an unrelated discussion.

Paul meant these verses to be an *application* of what he was talking about right before and right after. What he was talking about was loving neighbors and enemies. (Look it up and see for yourself!) In this discussion, Paul lays down at least two principles:

- "Don't repay evil for evil to a government that's persecuting you. Don't plan guerrilla raids against it. If you're tempted to think of your government as 'the enemy,' then remember what I say, what Jesus said—and what the Old Testament said, even—about how to treat enemies. In other words, overcome evil with good.

- "Remember, don't wrong a neighbor! In fact, you're even supposed to feed your *enemies.*"

When government wrongs us, we are not to wrong them in return. But what do we do when our government asks us to contradict the scriptural instruction to love our enemis? Sometimes we simply can't obey.

Civil Disobedience Versus Blind Obedience
(Acts 5:17-42)

The tradition of civil disobedience is a way of "not obeying" government when it asks us to violate scriptural principles, yet it also takes seriously the idea of submitting to authority. It involves *not trying to evade the consequences* of disobeying a law for conscience sake.

The first "civilly disobedient" Christians on record are Peter and his friends in Acts 5. After being thrown into jail for preaching, they told the authorities: "We must obey God rather than men."

At the other end of the spectrum from civil disobedience is something called blind obedience. Blind obedience can be a danger to a society—a disservice to one's country.

A psychologist named Stanley Milgram tried the

following experiment. He recruited some "average people" and told them to teach word-pairs to a group of "learners." The "teachers" thought the "learners" were average people just like themselves. Actually, the "learners" were trained actors who knew what the experiment was *really* about.

The method of "teaching" was to give the "learners" increasingly heavy electric shocks if they answered incorrectly. The "learners" didn't really receive the shocks, but pretended to—and screamed bloody murder.

Milgram told the "teachers" they were delivering dangerous 450-volt shocks which could cause death. The screams and pleas from the "learners" seemed to back that up. But still, 60 percent of the "teachers" kept on obeying orders.

Milgram's "teachers" were just ordinary people who obeyed orders. But so were the people who ran Germany's death camps during World War II. And so are the people who are trained to push levers at Strategic Air Command (SAC) bomber headquarters and on nuclear subs.

In our countries today, citizens support and pay for the arms race and prepare to fight wars just because the system demands it. We consider certain groups to be "enemies" just because of the way government officials talk. It often amounts to blind obedience.

It takes far more courage to buck the system than to go along with it. It takes far more courage to find the composer and play in his symphony. It takes far more courage to volunteer for the "army that sheds no blood."

Review and Reflect

1. Read Mark 12 and Romans 12, 13 for yourself. What ideas did you have about them before you read this chapter? Does this chapter's explanation make sense to you? Where *doesn't* it?

2. Comment on this statement: "The problem of the church has always been giving Caesar *more* than his due and giving God *less* than belongs to him."

3. Do you feel most comfortable with the first, second, or third God-and-Caesar diagram? Why?

4. Are emperor worship and worship of Mars, the god of war, alive today? Defend your answer!

5. Think about the words and music to your national anthem and other patriotic songs. How do they make you feel? How is that feeling the same as or different from the way you feel when you sing hymns in church?

6. Do you think a conscientious objector to war can be a good citizen? Why or why not? How about a person who withholds the war-related part of his or her income tax payment?

7. Why is the question of the Christian's obedience to government such a hot topic for people?

Books for (Very) Serious Study

Kehler, Larry. *The Rule of the Lamb.* Newton: Faith and Life Press, 1978.

Klaassen, Walter. *What Have You To Do with Peace?* Altona: D. W. Friesen, 1969. Chapters 1 and 8.

Yoder, John H. *The Politics of Jesus.* Grand Rapids: Eerdmans, 1972. Chapters 8 and 9.

8
What Can We Do About It?

I don't know about you, but I ain't gonna study war no more.
—Martin Luther King, Jr.

Maybe you've decided by now to join the army that sheds no blood. But you're just an ordinary person. We all are. So, realistically, what actions can we take to show that we're on the side of peace?

This chapter presents five issues that are staring ordinary peacemakers like us in the face today. They are: military service, career choice, war taxes, the buildup of nuclear weapons, and opportunities for peacemaking in our own communities.

It's hard for each of us to figure out exactly what kind of peacemaker God is calling us to be. But if we're serious about wanting to know, these five issues demand consideration. We'll look at them one by one.

The Right Not to Learn to Kill

The strongest action a person can take for peace is to say: "You're not going to train *me* for war. You're not going to force *me* to be a cog in your war machine. You're not going to get *my* body. I'm a conscientious objector to war!"

In 1976, seven Spanish conscientious objectors were jailed for their refusal to join the military. They issued this statement:

> We are only doing what we believe we must: oppose obligatory military service, as we can see no way (absolutely!) in which learning to kill serves the interests of peace. We ask the right to learn not to kill.

Conscientious objection to war is not a new thing. In fact, it was the normal position for a Christian to take in the Roman Empire for the first 300 years of Christian history.

Maximilian Resists the Draft

One of the first draft resisters we know by name was 21-year-old Maximilian, a North African conscript. Here are excerpts from his trial before Dion the Proconsul in 295 A.D.:

Dion: What is your name?

Maximilian: Why do you want to know my name?
I am not allowed to be a soldier; I am a
Christian

Dion: Measure him.

Assistant: Five feet, ten inches.

Dion: Put the badge on him.

Maximilian: I refuse. I cannot serve.

Dion: Be a soldier; otherwise you must die.

Maximilian: I will not be a soldier. . . . I have nothing to do with your badge. I already bear the sign of Christ my God. . . .

Dion: In the bodyguard of our lord Diocletian . . . there are Christian soldiers and they serve.

Maximilian: They know what they have to do. But I am a Christian and I cannot do what is evil.

Dion: But those who serve—what wrong do they do?

Maximilian: You know very well what they do. . . .

Dion: Strike his name off! Maximilian, out of insubordination, has refused the military oath and is therefore condemned to die by the sword.

Maximilian: God be praised!

Hutterite Martyrs at Fort Leavenworth

During World War I, four Hutterites were thrown into the "hole" at California's Alcatraz prison with the most hardened of criminals. (Hutterites, who live on communal farms, are plain people related to the Mennonites). For 1½ days they were handcuffed to a bar so high they could barely reach the floor. At night they shivered in their underwear on the cement floor. Every 24 hours they received only a half glass of water to drink and no food. After five days their skin was blotched with scurvy and insect bites.

All this happened because Jacob Wipf and the three Hofer brothers—Joseph, Michael, and David—were conscientious objectors who refused to put on a military uniform.

In November, 1918, after four months of harsh treatment, they were transferred to Fort Leavenworth, Kansas. Arriving at the prison late one night, they were forced to run up the hill to the gate until their hair was soaked with sweat.

Next, they were ordered to take off their clothes and wait in freezing temperature to receive prison issue. The new clothes didn't appear until two hours later. By morning, Joseph and Michael Hofer were in the prison hospital with pneumonia, both gravely ill.

Joseph's wife Maria arrived at the prison after his death. When she looked into his coffin, she saw that the prison officials had cruelly dressed Joseph in the military uniform he had refused to wear all along. Michael Hofer died a few days later.

After the funeral, their brother David was taken back to his cell. He remembers that the whole next day I stood there and wept. But I could not even dry my tears because my hands were chained to the iron bars of the prison.

David Hofer was released from prison several days later. But Jacob Wipf endured Leavenworth almost half a year longer, until his release in April 1919.

Maximilian, the Hofer Brothers, and Us

Christian history is strewn with martyrs like Maximilian and the Hofer brothers. But what about us? Canada has not had a draft since World War II. In the United States, the draft ended with the close of the Vietnam War. And during both World War II and the Vietnam War, conscientious-objector status was rather easy to get—at least if you were a member of one of the historic peace churches (Mennonite, Brethren, or Quaker).

But that doesn't mean we can ignore the question of our own involvement in the military. For instance, active recruitment for the Canadian Forces takes place in Canadian high schools. More than 60,000 Canadian high school kids are cadets, and 80 percent of Canadian military officers got their start as cadets in the school system.

At the beginning of the 80's, United States males were again being asked to register with the Selective Service System at the age of 18 for the possible reinstatement of a military draft.

It's a good idea for *all* of us Christian peacemakers— not just 18-year-old American males—to think through our response to a possible military draft. Some church denominations provide a Christian Peacemaker Registration Form for high schoolers to fill out and file at their church conference office. In the event of a draft, these people will be able to show that they already know what they believe as pacifists.

Christian Conscientious Objectors—Four Varieties

Christian conscientious objectors come in at least four varieties. Below is a brief description of each of these four positions. Which one do *you* identify with most closely? Do you know which one(s) your denomination supports?

Selective objection. Selective objectors operate from the just war theory. They believe that if their country is waging a just war, they have an obligation to fight in it. But if it's an unjust war, they have a Christian duty to refuse military participation. Many of the draft resisters from the late 60's were selective objectors who believed the Vietnam War was wrong.

Noncombatant military service. Some conscientious objectors believe they can be part of the military system as long as they aren't expected to actually kill people. These noncombatants go to military camps and may be asked to wear military uniforms. By providing backup services for combat troops, they symbolize their belief that God expects governments to engage in war.

Alternative service. Alternative service has been the traditional position of the historic peace churches. Conscientious objectors who enter alternative service believe they can best serve their country and the cause of peace by meeting human need when others are concentrating on war. Most of them believe that *all* war is against God's will.

During the last several decades, alternative service could be done through church agencies related to the historic peace churches. Jobs ranged from orderlies in mental hospitals to tutoring in the inner city to relief work in foreign countries.

Draft resistance—During the Vietnam era, a few conscientious objectors chose not to cooperate with the United States Selective Service System at all. Draft resister Dennis Koehn believes his role was like that of "a bicyclist who heads out into a storm to warn others of impending danger." The danger is what will happen to our world if we continue to depend on military solutions to our problems. You can read the stories of ten young men like Dennis in a book called *The Path of Most Resistance* (see listing at the end of this chapter).

Another application of this position is represented by young men in the United States who refuse to register with the Selective Service System. That this position is being considered more seriously by peace churches was evidenced by one group of nonregistrants appearing before a general assembly of a peace church. After these six young men made a case for nonregistration, they were given a standing ovation.

Choosing a Career That Promotes Life

Many of us are under no pressure to think about draft registration. But we all must think about career choices.

Joel Kauffmann, cartoonist for this book, believes that:

> Career options . . . are more important in relation to peace than they were 10 years ago. . . . The army of the future will consist of scientists, of civilians working for large corporations that provide military equipment, and there will be a very small number of actual military people.

In the 16th century, a Hutterite leader named Peter Riedemann clearly saw the connection between pacifism and how we make a living. He put it this way:

> Since Christians should beat their swords into ploughshares and take up arms no more . . . still less can they make the same. . . . Since Christians must not use and practice vengeance, neither can they make the weapons by which such vengeance and destruction may be practiced by others. . . . Therefore we make neither swords, spears, muskets, nor any such weapons.

All of us can work for peace by choosing a career that promotes life rather than one which destroys it.

Why Sandra Drescher Pays Only 50% of Her Taxes
According to *Sojourners* magazine, "The arms race would fall flat on its face if all the Christians who lament it would stop paying for it."

In recent years, an increasing number of Christians feel called to tax resistance. That is, they voluntarily pay only that part of their income tax which is not earmarked for military spending. They know their action is mostly a symbolic gesture—the government will get the money anyway. But tax resistance slows the bureaucratic system down a bit, and provides a way to witness about one's beliefs to a few government officials.

Again, the sixteenth century Hutterite leader Peter Riedemann explains the reason for tax resistance:

> Where taxes are demanded for the special purpose of going to war, massacring and shedding blood, we give nothing. This we do neither in malice or obstinacy, but in the fear of God that we make not ourselves partakers of other men's sins.

Sandra Drescher, author of *Just Between God and Me* (a devotional book for teens published by Zondervan), pays only half of her United States income tax. With her tax return, she includes a check for the other 50 percent—made out to Mennonite Central Committee "to help in the preservation of life." She also sends along a letter explaining her pacifist beliefs. One year it was signed by 38 people from her congregation.

Sandra's tax resistance started in 1978—the second year she earned enough money to pay income tax! One year her interaction with the Internal Revenue Service included eleven exchanges of letters and two phone calls.

To other peacemaking Christians, Sandra says:

> My primary purpose is . . . to be a witness for Jesus and to be the kind of servant I feel he wants me to be. . . . While I don't expect all of my Christian brothers and sisters to agree with my beliefs and actions, I pray that we can support one another as each of us patterns our life, as close as possible, to that of Jesus.

Christian peacemaking groups in both Canada and the United States are working to establish a World Peace Tax Fund. If Parliament and Congress eventually approve this alternate fund, conscientious objectors could legally pay the military-related portion of their tax monies into this fund which would then be used for human and social services. This way conscientious objectors would have an alternative to paying war taxes, just as they now have an alternative to military service.

I Want My Grandchildren to Live

A few Christians feel called to do drastic things to make others aware of the dangers of the arms race. Among them in 1980 were the Plowshares Eight.

The Plowshares Eight entered a General Electric manufacturing plant in eastern Pennsylvania early one morning, carrying tiny concealed hammers. Once in-

side the plant, they started "smashing" the nose cones of Mark 12A re-entry vehicles being assembled there. (Each Mark 12A carries a bomb 30 times more powerful than the one the U.S. dropped on Hiroshima.)

Next they pulled out baby bottles filled with their own blood and poured the blood over the blueprints they found. Then they prayed until police arrested them.

One of the participants was Molly Rush, a mother of six. Afterwards, Mrs. Rush said:

> I don't want to go to jail, but I don't know how to make people take me seriously. Life is what I'm all about. I want my grandchildren to live. . . . The most important way I felt I could love my family was to take the risks necessary to achieve a non-nuclear world.

Not all of us are called to this kind of civil disobedience. But all of us can at least inform ourselves—and people in our schools and churches—about what the arms race is doing to our world. (See the books listed at the end of chapter 5 and this chapter.)

According to historian Herbert Butterfield, the United States and the Soviet Union are acting like

> two criminals locked together in a prison cell. Each has a loaded

gun. Both want to see both guns thrown out of the window. But neither trusts the other enough to do it first.

More and more Christians are coming to believe that "the way to stop is to stop." These peacemakers advocate a nuclear "freeze"—a moratorium on the development and production of further nuclear weapons.

In 1981, various Christian groups also endorsed a World Peace Pledge which reads like this:

In the light of my faith, I am prepared to live without nuclear weapons in my country.

Thousands of citizens in the United States, Canada, Germany, Italy, Holland, Switzerland, and Great Britain have already signed this pledge.

Our democratic governments will, finally, do what they think we as citizens are asking them to do. Sometimes we need to tell them, "Hey, there are certain things I'm *not* asking you to do for me! 'Protecting' me with nuclear arms is one of them." Otherwise, how will our governments know?

Warman Versus Eldorado

War taxes, nuclear disarmament, even the military draft—all these can seem pretty remote from our day-to-day lives in Kitchener, Ontario, or Berne, Indiana, or Denver, Colorado. But often our contributions to peace come first by dealing with situations that arise at home.

Take Warman, Saskatchewan, for instance. Warman is a farming town where 70 percent of the people are Mennonite. In 1976, an agent hired by Eldorado Nuclear, Ltd., started approaching farmers around Warman about selling their land. Eldorado wanted to build a uranium refinery near Warman, Canada's third. The enriched uranium it produced would be exported for use in Canadian-made nuclear power reactors around the world.

Some farmers would have gotten rich by selling their land; the town would have prospered from the influx of workers. Maybe Warman could even have paved its main street!

But serious questions were raised by some people in the community. This was prime farmland, needed to grow food for Canada and the world. Also, the social fabric of the community would be broken if Eldorado came in. And would radioactive wastes be disposed of safely?

Anyway, Mennonites are opposed to war. So why would they sell their farms to give other countries the kind of uranium which can be used to make nuclear bombs?

There was a long battle, one which divided the community of Warman. But the refinery was kept out. Warman school principal Jake Buhler said:

> Many of us . . . felt for the first time in our lives that we had to defend who we were, what we believed, and why we believe as we do. One older gentleman told me, "Now you know how I felt during the second world war when I was asked to enlist in the army."

Reba Place Versus Three Teenage Thieves

Reba Place Fellowship is a Christian intentional community in the interracial Chicago suburb of Evanston, Illinois. In this urban environment, people inevitably steal things from Reba Place members sometimes. In an easy-to-read book called *Dial 911*, Dave Jackson tells how the community has handled such incidents.

One summer afternoon, Gary and Jan came home to find their back door open. The cash from the money jar was gone, and so was an old bread knife and some popsicles. Also, someone had turned the stereo speakers around.

Later that same day, Gary glimpsed three teenagers on the back porch. They saw him too and bolted. Gary ran till he caught up with one and persuaded the boy to come back to the house to talk.

Gary first explained to the fellow what it feels like to have one's house broken into and asked what had happened to the stash. (The boys ate the popsicles and bought hamburgers with the money.) Then Gary continued:

> All of these things are property of the church and therefore belong to God. I'm not necessarily wanting to protect them and keep them for myself. If you want some of these things, you're not free to take them, but you can ask for them. Then we can talk to some of the elders about who needs them most.

Gary decided not to call the police, and the fellow went home. But the next day the police came to see Gary anyway! The boy felt so guilty he told his mother, and she got furious enough to take him to the cops. The police were grateful for the chance to work with the parents in keeping these young teens on track.

A few days later, another boy dropped by to, as he said, "look at the stereo you're giving away." He turned out to be another of the petty thieves. What he really wanted was to apologize.

Plains Church Versus the Radio Preacher

One summer evening, a group of Russian Baptists came to speak at the Plains Mennonite Church outside the town of Lansdale, Pennsylvania. During the meeting, a local radio preacher and some followers picketed the church. The radio preacher believed the Russian Baptists were communist spies; so in his eyes, the organizers of the meeting must be "soft on communism."

It was a terribly hot evening. The people inside the church were hot, and so were the picketers outside. What should the members of Plains Church do?

Some of them decided to go out and talk to the picketers. They accompanied their talk with a symbolic action. They set up a table and offered drinks of cold water.

The Plains Church people wanted to show the picketers that they bore no ill will. They remembered Paul's advice: "If your enemy is thirsty, give him a drink."

Review and Reflect

1. Find out about the experiences of relatives or family friends who were conscientious objectors during war-time—or who served in the military. What do they think now?

2. Imagine that you personally (whether you're Canadian, female, or whatever!) have to face a military draft tomorrow. What would you say and do?

3. What career are you projecting for yourself? How does it help to promote—or destroy—life?

4. Do you know of someone who is a war tax resister? Offer him or her your support—or explain why you can't.

5. How would you react if a member of Plowshares Eight came to speak at your school?

6. What opportunities for peacemaking have arisen in your community lately? What have you done about them?

7. What have you done to inform yourself and others about the dangers of the nuclear arms race?

Books for (Very) Serious Study

A Matter of Faith: A Study Guide for Churches on the Nuclear Arms Race. Washington: Sojourners, 1981.

Clouse, Robert G., ed. *War: Four Christian Views*. Downers Grove: InterVarsity Press, 1981.

Jackson, Dave. *Dial 911: Peaceful Christians and Urban Violence*. Scottdale: Herald Press, 1981.

Kauffmann, Joel. *The Weight*. Scottdale: Herald Press, 1980. (A novel about turning 18 in a Mennonite community during the Vietnam War. Watch for the film version too!)

Miller, Melissa, and Shenk, Phil M. *The Path of Most Resistance*. Scottdale: Herald Press, 1982.

Seeley, Robert A. *Handbook for Conscientious Objectors*. Philadelphia: Central Committee for Conscientious Objectors, 1981.

Sider, Ronald and Taylor, Richard. *Christians in a Nuclear Age*. Downers Grove: InterVarsity Press, 1982.

Film

Every Heart Beats True. Produced by Packard Manse Media Project (1980, 20 minutes), it traces Christian pacifism from Jesus to Maximilian to the present. The film shows that teenage Christian pacifists in any denomination can find support.

9
Eleven Facts About Peacemakers

Christ has no body now on earth but yours, no hands but yours, no feet but yours.

—*Teresa of Avila*

Peacemaking is a complex matter. So here, in summary, are eleven statements about how peacemakers think and behave. They bring together many of the strands of thought woven into this book.

Compare your own beliefs and actions with these "facts about peacemakers." Are *you* a peacemaker?

1. Peacemakers Preserve the Earth
(Deuteronomy 30:19)

In the Old Testament book of Deuteronomy, Moses says to the Israelites as they're about to enter the Promised Land:

> I have set before you life and death, blessing and curse; therefore choose life, that you and your descendants may live.

The choice between life and death—between preserving the world and destroying it—is set before us very starkly these days.

We saw (in chapter 1) that humanity is supposed to act as God's agent in preserving the earth. We've also seen how the arms race threatens the whole earth.

We humans now have the know-how to let our "Cain instinct" put an end to it all. But God hasn't reversed his orders in the meantime. The command to "preserve the earth" still stands, and peacemakers are the ones obeying it.

2. Peacemakers Understand How Things Connect

Many people like to think their country can look out for its own interests in the world and "let the chips fall where they may." But it can't.

That's because we live in an interdependent world where we connect with everybody else. Our planet is "spaceship earth." A peacemaker named Robert McAfee Brown puts it like this:

> Everybody is in the act together. No one can be ignored. The entire mission is threatened if there is a mutiny among the crew.

Maybe Christians can understand the idea of global connections better than some other people. The church is, after all, a global network. Because we belong to the church, we already have a way of thinking about humankind in global terms.

In fact, a good way to learn about how the world interconnects is to listen to returned church workers from overseas. They're a good source of information about what's going on in the world. The "global network" of returned missionaries and "Christian service" workers can help to balance what the State Department and External Affairs tell us.

Our world spends $500,000,000,000 on military forces and weapons each year. That's a stack of $1000 bills 50 miles high! For the cost of just one new MX missile, 50,000,000 children in developing countries could be properly fed. For the cost of one tank, 30,000 classrooms could be built. And for the cost of one fighter plane, basic medical care could be provided for 40,000 people.

Our world simply can't do everything at once.

3. *Peacemakers Feed the Hungry*
(Romans 12:20; Matthew 25:31-46)

U.S. Senator Mark Hatfield believes that

the greatest threat to the stability of the entire world is hunger. It's more explosive than all the atomic weaponry possessed by the great powers. Desperate people do desperate things.

Evangelist Billy Graham puts the question like this:

Is it God's will that resources be used for massive armaments which could otherwise be used for alleviating human suffering and hunger? Of course not. Our world has lost sight of true values.

A basic command of the New Testament is to feed the hungry—whether he is the enemy or not. Jesus even says that feeding the hungry is a service to him. But the hungry cannot be fed—in North America or elsewhere—as long as our governments spend this much money on armaments. They cannot be fed as long as we in North America are this greedy of the world's bananas, oil, and cobalt.

Christians who are aware of these connections and vow to live on less now are making a big contribution to peace.

4. *Peacemakers Pray for Peace*
(1 Timothy 2:1, 2)

When Paul writes to Timothy about how to conduct public worship, he says:

My advice is that, first of all, there should be prayers offered for everyone—petitions, intercessions and thanksgiving—and especially for kings and others in authority, so that we may be able to live religious and reverent lives in peace and quiet (JB).

Now the idea of praying may seem to contradict what we've been talking about. Praying seems like such a passive response to war and conflict. And the world has massive problems which demand *action!* So praying seems like an easy way to get out of our responsibility. Just mumble a quick prayer and that's it!

But that's not it, at all. Mahatma Gandhi, who led India's nonviolent campaign for independence, put it like this:

Prayer is not an old woman's idle amusement. Properly understood and applied, it is the most potent instrument of action.

Have you ever consciously prayed for somebody you're quarreling with? Try it sometime! It quickly goads you to action. If you really start praying for somebody, you can't help thinking about them and taking their concerns seriously.

When we pray for peace, it leads to respect for the difficult job government has to do—and to more clear thinking about our own involvement.

PONTIUS' PUDDLE

TWINKLE TWINKLE HEAVENLY SPHERE, HOW I WONDERED WHAT YOU WERE. BEACONING HOPE FROM HIGH ABOVE, A REMINDER OF CELESTIAL LOVE--

Prayer also helps us remember who we are—God's children. It helps us regain our confidence that the world is in God's hands. Jim Wallis, editor of *Sojourners* magazine, says:

> Prayer declares who we are and to whom we belong.... Prayer changes our frame of reference.... Prayer is not undertaken instead of other actions but as the foundation for all the rest of the actions we take.

5. *Peacemakers Look Toward God's Future*
(See Chapter 4)

Christian peacemakers realize that our world is in a timewarp. We live in an era of overlapping time dimensions. In one sense, it's the same old evil world out there. But at the same time, something wonderful has started to happen; we in the church have been let in on the secret.

God's kingdom is growing like a mustard seed. Jesus showed through his life, death, and resurrection what God's way to peace is. When we are peacemakers, we demonstrate our belief that Jesus has shown God's way.

Our actions for peace are little signs that we know God's secret. Since they come out of a timewarp, they sometimes seem out of sync with the rest of what's go-

THE TIME HAS COME POLITICIANS SAY,
TO EQUIP YOU WITH A DEADLY RAY,
TWINKLE TWINKLE HEAVENLY SPHERE,
I USED TO WONDER--NOW I FEAR.

ing on. That's why one writer has called them "signs of contradiction" which give people hope. Our actions for peace say to people: "What you see around you is not all there is."

A good example of this kind of thinking came in Italy in the 1930's, when the fascist dictator Mussolini forced people to join his army. In one town in Sicily, a schoolteacher posted a sign on a public bulletin board saying he would not join the army because the fascists were wrong. As he was taken out to be shot the next day, someone asked him, "Why did you place the notice on the town hall when you knew it would not do any good?"

The man's answer: "I did not want it to be unanimous."

The schoolteacher's note—and his death—were not useless. They gave people a glimpse of eternal values, and allowed them to hope that Mussolini wouldn't last forever.

6. *Peacemakers Believe Death Is Not the End*

In other words, pacifists know that their methods don't always bring immediate results. People who are brought face to face with the utter senselessness of violence often become the most committed pacifists.

This is how one such person—now a retired minister in Canada—became a pacifist:

Isaac Tiessen was a young Mennonite boy living in the Molotschna village in Russia in 1918. It was a time of anarchy, when people never really knew who was in charge. First the czarist White Army would come sweeping through the Mennonite villages, threatening to kill young men if they didn't join the troops. Then the communist Red Army would come through and do the same.

Young Isaac saw his two older brothers ordered at

gunpoint to join the Red Army. When they refused, Isaac watched as the soldiers shot them to death. Suddenly, the boy realized that if he had been old enough, he too would have refused to join either army.

Isaac became a pacifist in that moment. In that very worst of situations, he came to the firm belief that death is not the last word.

Evangelist Myron Augsburger believes:

> He [Jesus] showed us that we do not have to live; we can die. In dying we may sometimes do more for enriching the world than we would have done by living.

7. *Peacemakers Stay Out of the Enemy's Sewer*
(Mark 3:23)

John Hersey's novel, *The Wall*, is based on one of the most heroic struggles in recent history—the battle by Jewish street fighters against Nazi tanks and battalions in the Warsaw ghetto in the spring of 1943.

At the end, after the Nazis had completely razed the ghetto, a few remaining street fighters huddled in a sewer pipe for 30 hours, waiting to be rescued. In the sewer, two of Hersey's characters have this conversation:

> *Rachel:* So far as the rest of our religion is concerned, I think there is only one thing: not to hurt anybody.... Thou shalt love thy neighbor as thyself.
> *Noach:* Even if thy neighbor is a Nazi?
> *Rachel:* How else cure him of being a Nazi?
> *Noach:* Maybe there is no cure. Maybe you have to kill him.
> *Rachel:* I've tried that, and where did it get me? Where am I now?
> *Noach:* In a sewer.

Armed resistance seemed the only way for Rachel and Noach to show the Nazis they were human. And yet they learned that "to kill rather than cure with love draws one into the enemy's sewer."

In other words, how can love and peace result from the use of violence? How can thistle seeds produce apples? Or, as Jesus asked it, "How can Satan cast out Satan?" It just doesn't work that way!

Christian pacifists want to point out God's way of peace wherever and however they can. The problem with all other ways to peace is that we end up in the enemy's sewer.

8. *Peacemakers Come in Many Styles*
(Matthew 5:13-15)

Christian peacemakers often ask: How active should our peacemaking be, anyway? Should we form separate communities to model what God has in mind for people? Or should we plunge right into society and work to bring about peace that way?

The answer is: both. Some individuals and groups of Christian peacemakers focus on one side of it; some on the other. In different situations, the same individual or group will lean toward one side or the other.

Unfortunately, Christian peacemakers waste a lot of energy calling each other names over different styles of peacemaking. Activist peacemakers tend to think of conservative Mennonite and Amish groups as "irrelevant" and "naive." And peacemakers who don't get politically involved tend to call activists "compromisers" who "aren't even Christian."

Groups of peacemakers who separate themselves from society are like the "city on the hill" Jesus mentions in the Sermon on the Mount. The most important thing about a city on a hill is simply that it's *there*. People can look at it, grope towards it, and use it to find their way. It provides that safe feeling you get when you come over the last hill and—ah—there are the lights of your town, your city, or your farmhouse.

There's a science fiction novel called *The Long*

Tomorrow, set in eastern Ohio after a nuclear holocaust. In it, everybody is required by law to live like the Old Order Amish! As the novelist implies, the Amish are not irrelevant at all. In fact, they're the only people self-sufficient enough to survive.

But most of us are not like the Old Order Amish. We're much more assimilated into society. We're more like the "salt of the earth" in the Sermon on the Mount.

Salt is noticeable in a different way from a city on a hill. You can't see salt, but it's there, permeating things. And its presence is felt most at the moment it enters a new substance. Salty Christian peacemakers make their communities—and the world—better places for us all.

9. *Peacemakers Start with the Church*

Try picturing things like this: the church is at the center and the "world" (our society, including government) is around it.

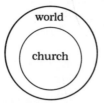

We start by being in the church—by modeling among ourselves the new humanity that God has in mind as long as the world continues. We help each other to see and live God's way of peace. We look for connections. We show people alternatives to what they see around them.

Then, we move out from there. Some peacemakers believe that the extent to which you get involved in the rest of the world depends on how far society allows you to go. You get as involved as possible without destroying your principles.

And the principles of well-intentioned Christian peacemakers are not going to be identical. So we need to respect each other—and to challenge each other to test out our beliefs and actions with a community of faith.

Remember André Trocmé, the French Protestant pastor from chapter 2? During the 1940's, he participated in local government in a way which he called "the politics of repentance."

Trocmé believed that "a Christian should be ready to take part in government as long as it will let one continue to be Christian." But you also need to be "ready to withdraw or be removed" when the government asks you to do something opposed to your conscience.

Trocmé was removed twice—once by the Nazis for not handing over fleeing Jews, and then later by the French for not handing over Nazi sympathizers.

10. Peacemakers Don't Say, "How Terrible"

One thing is certain. Peacemaking never means standing back at a safe distance and saying, "How terrible!" It always involves taking risks; it always requires action.

The New Testament describes our vocation of peacemaking in phrases like this:

- seek peace and pursue it (1 Peter 3:11);
- pursue what makes for peace (Romans 14:19);
- so far as it depends upon you, live peaceably with all (Romans 12:18);
- be at peace among yourselves (1 Thessalonians 5:13);
- take the whole armor of God . . . having shod your feet with the equipment of the gospel of peace
  (Ephesians 6:13, 15).

All these phrases imply action; all of them require work. To "be at peace among yourselves" may be the hardest command of all!

You may have heard these words from Handel's *Messiah* (courtesy of the prophet Isaiah):

> How beautiful upon the mountain
>   are the feet of him who brings good tidings,
> who publishes peace.
>
>   Isaiah 52:7

To publish peace! How active can you get?

11. Peacemakers Leave the Result to God

Teresa of Avila, a Christian writer from the sixteenth century, said: "Christ has no body now on earth but yours, no hands but yours, no feet but yours." We are Christ's agents for peace, his body on earth.

But we are only his agents—we are not in control of the process. We work for peace, but we don't claim the credit for bringing it about. We are orchestra members with stunning parts, but we're not the composer.

Thomas Merton, a twentieth century monk, put it like this:

> The big results are not in your hands or mine, but they suddenly happen, and we can share in them.

To be "success-oriented" in peacemaking can be a fatal flaw. We don't know God's timetable. We *do* know that it takes decades for an orchard of apples to grow from seed.

We don't know whether the end of the world will come through a nuclear holocaust or some other way. We don't know *what* will happen—to the world or to us. We don't have all the answers. But we do know that whatever happens, God is and will be faithful.

No matter what happens, the instruction we have is to keep on preserving the earth and to do it in the way Jesus set out for us. In other words, we should be a sign of God's future that is coming, actively working for peace with the knowledge that the result is safely in God's hands.

Review and Reflect

1. Where do you agree and disagree with the "eleven facts about peacemakers"? Are you a peacemaker?

2. Look up Jesus' job description in Luke 4:18-19. How active was his peacemaking?

3. Martin Luther King said: "There is always a third option between doing nothing and resorting to violence. The problem is finding those options and acting on them." What do you think?

4. Read the three "think pieces" and the prayer following this chapter. What do they add to your understanding of Christian peacemaking?

Books for (Very) Serious Study

Brown, Robert McAfee. *Making Peace in the Global Village.* Philadelphia: Westminster Press, 1981.

Grannis, Christopher, et. al. *The Risk of the Cross: Christian Discipleship in the Nuclear Age.* New York: Seabury Press, 1981.

Keeney, William. *Lordship as Servanthood.* Newton: Faith and Life Press, 1975.

Koontz, Ted and Gayle, et. al. *Which Lord?* Scottdale: *Youth Bible Studies,* 1974.

Longacre, Doris. *Living More with Less.* Scottdale: Herald Press, 1980.

The Peacemaker. Newton: Faith and Life Press and Scottdale: Mennonite Publishing House, 1972.

PONTIUS' PUDDLE
HOW CAN YOU JUSTIFY SPENDING BILLIONS ON ELABORATE WEAPON SYSTEMS WHEN MILLIONS ARE HOMELESS AND HUNGRY.
I ASSURE YOU THAT MY POLICIES TAKE THAT CONCERN INTO ACCOUNT.
ARE YOU PROJECTING AN INCREASE IN THE AMOUNT OF FOOD AND SHELTER?
NO, A DECREASE IN THE NUMBER OF CREATURES AROUND TO NEED IT.

Notes

The major sources for the views presented in this book are listed in the "Books for (Very) Serious Study" sections at the end of each chapter.

These notes are here so interested readers will know where to look for more complete versions of some of the stories and quotes found in the book.

Chapter 1. Peace, Peace: If God Wants It, Why Isn't There Any?

The true story of Mr. Wesley is reprinted in full from *Erie Christian Witness* in *A Race to Nowhere: An Arms Race Primer for Catholics* (Pax Christi, 1981).

The quote from Henry Wright is found in Barbara Habenstreit's *Men Against War* (Doubleday, 1973), a history of pacifism in America in easy-to-read story form.

John Woolman's observation that our treasure, furniture, and garments might "nourish the seeds of war" comes from his journal, *The Journal and Major Essays of John Woolman* (Oxford University, 1971). Woolman's journal gives fascinating insights into Quaker life in colonial America. Here was a man who really understood how things connect!

Chapter 2. What Jesus Said About Enemies

The story of the Good Mexican owes much to Clarence Jordan. Also, two quotes in the chapter ("if you bomb us, we'll obliterate you" and "love your own group and hate the hostile outsider") are from Jordan's *The Substance of Faith* (Association, 1972).

For the complete story of Earl Martin in Vietnam, see his *Reaching the Other Side* (Crown, 1978). The quote about Earl and Pat being "mother and father to all children" comes from the Sunday school quarterly *Which Lord?* (Herald Youth Bible Studies, 1974).

André Trocmé's example comes to light in Philip Haillie's *Lest In-*

nocent Blood Be Shed (Harper, 1979); "How William Rotch Resisted the Privateers" is rewritten from one of Elizabeth Bender's peace stories in *Coals of Fire* (Herald Press, 1954).

Chapter 3. What Jesus Did About Enemies

These stories are straight from the New Testament!

Chapter 4. Joining the Army That Sheds No Blood

The "someone" who said "evil feeds upon itself" is Walter Klaassen in *What Have You to Do with Peace?* (D. W. Friesen, 1969). Clarence Jordan's update of Paul again comes from *The Substance of Faith.* The pledge of allegiance to the cross is reprinted from *Which Lord?*

All quotes from Myron Augsburger in this book are from *War: Four Christian Views* (Robert Clouse, ed., InterVarsity, 1981). "Never mind, Lord, I'll do it myself" comes from William Robert Miller's *Nonviolence: A Christian Interpretation* (Association Press, 1964).

Dorothy Day's ironic comparison of war and the gospel is quoted in Richard McSorley's excellent *New Testament Basis of Peacemaking* (Center for Peace Studies, 1979). If you're going to buy just one book on war and the gospel, make it McSorley's (after mine!).

Mark Twain's "War Prayer" is part of a fine collection of peace poetry, fiction, and essays called *Enough of Dying!* (ed. Kay Boyle and Justine Van Gundy, Dell, 1972).

Also useful in this chapter was the *Youth Bible Studies,* "Suffer as Christ Suffered," "Love as Christ Loved," "Serve as Christ Served," and "Forgive as Christ Forgave" (Mennonite Publishing House and Faith and Life Press, 1979) by Robert Zuercher.

Chapter 5. Isn't Violence Sometimes the Only Way?

"If you start a person killing, you can't turn him off again like an engine" is quoted by Alan Kreider and John H. Yoder in "Christians and War" (*Eerdman's Handbook to the History of Christianity,* Eerdmans, 1977). This article provides a concise, easy-to-read summary of pacifism, the just war and the crusade in Christian history. For a more in-depth study, see Roland Bainton's *Christian Attitudes toward War and Peace* (Abingdon, 1960).

See George Zabelka's story in the August, 1980, issue of *Sojourners* magazine ("I Was Told It Was Necessary"). The "experts' predictions" of the effects of nuclear war come from *CBS Reports,* Ernie Regehr's *Militarism and the World Military Order* (World Council of Churches, 1980), and Richard McSorley's *Kill for Peace?* (Corpus, 1970).

A fuller account of the Norwegian resistance can be found in Miller's *Nonviolence: A Christian Interpretation* (Association Press, 1964) or Klaassen's *What Have You To Do With Peace?* (D. W. Friesen, 1969). Sources for "The Case of the Tired Seamstress" include *Nonviolence: A Christian Interpretation,* Habenstreit's *Men Against War* and Cornelia Lehn's *Peace Be With You* (Faith and Life, 1981). The latter contains 59 stories of Christian peacemakers from the first century to the twentieth, suitable for use in family or church settings.

The quote in question 5 is from James W. Douglass' *The Non-Violent Cross* (Macmillan, 1966). Question 6 comes from Robert McAfee Brown's *Making Peace in the Global Village* (Westminster, 1981).

Chapter 6. What About War in the Old Testament?

The argument of this chapter is based on the four authors listed at the end, especially Lind and Craigie. I am also indebted to Marion Bontrager of Hesston College for the term "remedial will of God" and for the illustration of the tall graceful vase and the squatty flowerpot.

Chapter 7. Aren't We Supposed to Obey the Government?

"Keep Off the Grass—A Quiz" is reprinted from *Youth Bible Study Guide* (Mennonite Publishing House and Faith and Life Press, June-August, 1981). The God-Caesar diagrams 1a and 3 come from Klaassen's *What Have You to Do with Peace?*

The discussion of "Tiberius and the Laurel Wreath" owes much to Willard Swartley's analysis in *Peace Section Newsletter* (Mennonite Central Committee, January-February, 1981) entitled "What does the New Testament Say About War Taxes?" Stanley Milgram's experiment is written up in more detail in Larry Kehler's *The Rule of the Lamb* (Faith and Life, 1978).

Chapter 8. What Can We Do About It?

The excerpts from Maximilian's trial come from McSorley's *New Testament Basis of Peacemaking.* "The Martyrdom of Joseph and Michael Hofer" is translated from *Das Klein-Geschichtsbuch der Hutterischen Brüder* and duplicated for classroom use at Associated Mennonite Biblical Seminaries.

Joel Kauffmann's quote about career choice is from an interview in the May, 1981, issue of *With* magazine, "Peace Means Relating to People" (Herald Press and Faith and Life Press). For more on Sandra Drescher's tax resistance, see the April, 1981, issue of *Christian Living* magazine, "What Shall I Do With My 1980 Income Tax Return?" (Mennonite Publishing House). For more of Molly Rush's story, see the July, 1981, issue of *Christian Living,* "I Want My Children to Live."

Chapter 9. Eleven Facts About Peacemakers

The story of the schoolteacher in Sicily is from McSorley's *Kill for Peace?* The story of Isaac Tiessen is recounted by John Rempel. The quote from Hersey's *The Wall* and the observation that "to kill ... draws one into the enemy's sewer" come from Douglass' *The Non-Violent Cross.*

The science fiction novel set in eastern Ohio in which all people are required by law to live like the Amish following a nuclear holocaust is *The Long Tomorrow* by Leigh Brackett (Ballantine, 1975).

The source for the church-world diagram and related discussion is the Koontz' *Which Lord?*

PONTIUS' PUDDLE

I WONDER IF GOD CAN REALLY HEAR ME.

HEY, GOD! WHAT SHOULD I DO WITH MY LIFE?

FEED THE HUNGRY. RIGHT INJUSTICE. WORK FOR PEACE!

JUST TESTING!

SAME HERE!

APPENDICES

**Six Reasons Why Peacemakers
Are Persecuted**

1. They get in the middle of things and some of the blows accidently land on them.
2. They often take the side of the most oppressed, such as the black in America, bringing the anger of the other side upon them.
3. They advocate a nonmilitary policy which threatens the military-industrial establishment.
4. They have an international rather than nationalistic outlook.
5. They themselves refuse to use military weapons as a means of solving differences.
6. They believe in feeding the enemy as well as the friend regardless of political consequences.

Are you a peacemaker?

—From *The Peacemaker*, Faith and Life Press and Mennonite Publishing House, 1972, p. 56.

A Prayer for the Reader

Lord, make me an instrument of Thy peace.
Where there is hatred, let me sow love;
Where there is injury, pardon;
Where there is doubt, faith.
Where there is despair, hope;
Where there is darkness, light;
Where there is sadness, joy.
O Divine Master, grant that I may not so much seek
To be consoled, as to console;
To be understood, as to understand;
To be loved, as to love.
For it is in giving that we receive;
It is in pardoning that we are pardoned;
It is in dying that we are born to eternal life.

—Attributed to Francis of Assisi, a Christian peacemaker from the 13th century

Then There Is Only One Choice

You, machine worker, and man in the workshop. Tomorrow, when they order you no longer to make water pipes and cooking ware but steel helmets and machine artillery; then there is only one choice: say no!

You, young lady behind the sales counter, and girl in the office. Tomorrow, when they order you to fill grenades and mount telescope sights for machine guns; then there is only one choice: say no!

You, researcher in the laboratory. Tomorrow, when they order you to discover a new death for this old life; then there is only one choice: say no!

You, poet in your study. Tomorrow, when they order you to sing songs of hate instead of songs of love; then there is only one choice: say no!

You, minister in your pulpit. Tomorrow, when they order

you to bless murder and to sanctify war; then there is only one choice: say no!

You, captain of a steamer. Tomorrow, when they order you no longer to haul wheat, but rather, cannon and panzers; then there is only one choice: say no!

You, man in the village and man in the city. Tomorrow, when they come to bring you an enlistment order; then there is only one choice: say no!

You, mother in Normandy, mother in the Ukraine. You, mother in Frisco and London. Mothers from all parts of the world. Tomorrow, when they order you to bear children, nurses for infirmaries and soldiers for new slaughters; mothers of the world, then there is only one choice: say no!

—From *Arena* magazine, December, 1967, p. 8. Wolfgang Borchart, author; translated from German by John Rempel.

The Weight of Nothing

"Tell me the weight of a snowflake," a coal-mouse asked a wild dove.

"Nothing more than nothing," was the answer.

"In that case I must tell you a marvelous story," the coal-mouse said. "I sat on the branch of a fir, close to its trunk, when it began to snow, not heavily, not in a raging blizzard, no, just like in a dream, without any violence. Since I didn't have anything better to do, I counted the snowflakes settling on the twigs and needles of my branch. Their number was exactly 3,741,952. When the next snowflake dropped onto the branch—nothing more than nothing, as you say—the branch broke off."

Having said that, the coal-mouse flew away.

The dove, since Noah's time an authority on the matter, thought about the story for a while and finally said to herself: "Perhaps there is only one person's voice lacking for peace to come about in the world."

—From *A Race to Nowhere: An Arms Race Primer for Catholics,* Mary Lou Kownacki, ed., Pax Christi USA (1981), 3000 N. Mango Ave., Chicago, Ill. 60634.

PONTIUS' PUDDLE

For More Information

Here is a list of organizations which can help you be a peacemaker in your own Christian tradition.

Historic Peace Churches
Mennonite Central Committee
   Peace Section
21 S. 12 St.
Akron, Pa. 17501
In Canada:
   201-1483 Pembina Hwy.
   Winnipeg, Man. R3T 2C8

New Call to Peacemaking
Box 1245
Elkhart, Ind. 46515

Church of the Brethren
World Ministries Commission
1451 Dundee Ave.
Elgin, Ill. 60120

American Friends Service
   Committee
1501 Cherry St.
Philadelphia, Pa. 19102
In Canada:
   Canadian Friends Service
      Committee
   60 Lowther Ave.
   Toronto, Ont. M5R 1C7

Evangelical
Baptist Peacemaker
Deer Park Baptist Church
1733 Bardstown Rd.
Louisville, Ky. 40205

Sojourners
1309 L Street NW
Washington, D.C. 20005

Catholic
Pax Christi—USA
3000 N. Mango Ave.
Chicago, Ill. 60634

Canadian Catholic Organization
   for Development and Peace
67 Bond St.
Toronto, Ont. M5B 1X4

Protestant
The American Lutheran Church
Division for Service and Mission
   in America
231 Madison Ave.
New York, N.Y. 10016

Reformed Church in America
General Program Council
475 Riverside Dr. Room 1809
New York, N.Y. 10115

United Methodist Church
Board of Church and Society
100 Maryland Ave. NE
Washington, D.C. 20002

United Church of Canada
Division of Mission
85 St. Clair Ave. E.
Toronto, Ont. M4T 1M8

Inter-Church
Central Committee for
   Conscientious Objectors
   (CCCO)
2208 South St.
Philadelphia, Pa. 19146

Fellowship of Reconciliation
Box 271
Nyack, N.Y. 10960

National Interreligious Service
   Board for Conscientious
   Objectors (NISBCO)
550 Washington Building
15 St. and New York Ave. NW
Washington, D.C. 20005

Project Plowshares
Conrad Grebel College
Waterloo, Ont. N2L 3G6

Index of Scriptures Cited

Troyer Studio

The Author

Susan (Sue) Clemmer Steiner grew up in Souderton, Pennsylvania. Her writing career began at Christopher Dock Mennonite High School, where she edited the *Dockument* (school newspaper).

After high school, Sue spent four busy years in Goshen, Indiana. She edited the Goshen College *Record*, and graduated with a BA in English in 1969. She also met Sam Steiner, a Mennonite draft resister. They were married in Canada in August 1969 and now live in Waterloo, Ontario.

From 1969-79, Sue bought general and children's books for the Provident Bookstores in Ontario, and also wrote many of Provident's ads. Browsing in bookstores is still a favorite pastime for Sue and her husband (who is a librarian!).

Sue has enjoyed teaching Sunday school to high schoolers and serving as youth sponsor at Rockway Mennonite Church in Kitchener, where she is a member. Her writings for teens have been published in *With* magazine and in the *Youth Bible Study Guide*. She has also written for the *Mennonite Reporter*, *Christian Living*, *Gospel Herald* and *On the Line*.

Sue attended Waterloo Lutheran Seminary, Waterloo, Ontario, and holds the MDiv degree from Associated Mennonite Biblical Seminaries, Elkhart, Indiana. Her service has included being the youth minister for the Mennonite Conference of Ontario and later a pastor of the St. Jacobs Mennonite Church.

The Cartoonist

Joel Kaufmann's puddle is Goshen, Indiana, where he lives with his wife Nancy, and their two tadpoles, Justin and Julian. Nancy is youth and young adult pastor at College Mennonite Church.

Joel is author of *The Best of Sisters and Brothers*, a collection of cartoons and humorous short stories, and *The Weight*, a serious novel about an eighteen-year-old with a very serious problem—the Draft (Herald Press, 1980).

Joel worked with a group of Mennonite film makers to produce a movie based on *The Weight*.

The Christian Peace Shelf

The Christian Peace Shelf is a selection of Herald Press books and pamphlets devoted to the promotion of Christian peace principles and their applications. The editor (appointed by the Mennonite Central Committee Peace Section) and an editorial board from the Brethren in Christ Church, the General Conference Mennonite Church, the Mennonite Brethren Church, and the Mennonite Church, represent the historic concern for peace within these constituencies.

FOR SERIOUS STUDY

Durland, William R. *No King But Caesar?* (1975). A Catholic lawyer looks at Christian violence.

Enz, Jacob J. *The Christian and Warfare* (1972). The roots of pacifism in the Old Testament.

Hershberger, Guy F. *War, Peace, and Nonresistance* (Third Edition, 1969). A classic comprehensive work on nonresistance in faith and history.

Hornus, Jean-Michael. *It Is Not Lawful for Me to Fight* (1980). Early Christian attitudes toward war, violence, and the state.

Kaufman, Donald D. *What Belongs to Caesar?* (1969). Basic arguments against voluntary payment of war taxes.

Lasserre, Jean. *War and the Gospel* (1962). An analysis of Scriptures related to the ethical problem of war.

Lind, Millard C. *Yahweh Is a Warrior* (1980). The theology of warfare in ancient Israel.

Ramseyer, Robert L. *Mission and the Peace Witness* (1979). Implications of the biblical peace testimony for the evangelizing mission of the church.

Trocmé, André. *Jesus and the Nonviolent Revolution* (1973). The social and political relevance of Jesus.

Yoder, John H. *The Original Revolution* (1972). Essays on Christian pacifism.

_____. *Nevertheless* (1971). The varieties and shortcomings of Christian pacifism.

FOR EASY READING

Barrett, Lois. *The Way God Fights* (1987). How the Old Testament points toward the New.

Beachey, Duane. *Faith in a Nuclear Age* (1983) A Christian response to war.

Byler, Dennis. *Making War and Making Peace* (1989). Why some Christians fight and some don't.

Drescher, John M. *Why I Am a Conscientious Objector* (1982). A personal summary of basic issues for every Christian facing military involvements.

Driver, John. *How Christians Made Peace with War* (1988). How Christians in the early church became involved in the military.

Eller, Vernard. *War and Peace from Genesis to Revelation* (1981). Explores peace as a consistant theme developing throughout the Old and New Testaments.

Hostetler, Marian. *They Loved Their Enemies* (1988). True stories of African Christians who nonviolently faced a conflict.

Kaufman, Donald D. *The Tax Delemma: Praying for Peace, Paying for War* (1978). Biblical, historical, and practical considerations on the war tax issue.

Kraybill, Donald B. *Facing Nuclear War* (1982). A plea for Christian witness.

_____. *The Upside-Down Kingdom* (1978, 1990). A study of the synoptic Gospels on the affluence, war-making, status-seeking, and religious exclusivism.

Miller, John W. *The Christian Way* (1969). A guide to the Christian life based on the Sermon on the Mount.

Sider, Ronald J. *Christ and Violence* (1979). A sweeping reappraisal of the church's teaching on violence.

Steiner, Susan Clemmer. *Joining the Army That Sheds No Blood* (1982). The case for biblical pacifism written for teens.

Stoner, John K., and Lois Barrett. *Letters to American Christians* (1989). Jesus' teachings compared with evangelicalism and militarism.

Wenger, J.C. *The Way of Peace* (1977). A brief treatment on Christ's teachings and the way of peace through the centuries.

Yoder, John H. *What Would You Do?* (1983). Responses to—What would you do if someone was attacking your sister?

FOR CHILDREN

Bauman, Elizabeth Hershberger. *Coals of Fire* (1954). Stories of people who returned good for evil.

Eitzen, Ruth. *The White Feather* (1987). A picture storybook on making peace with Indian neighbors.

Moore, Joy Hofacker. *Ted Studebaker: A Man Who Loved Peace* (1987). Picture storybook about a peace hero who went to Vietnam as a teacher.

Moore, Ruth Nulton, *Peace Treaty* (1977). A historical novel involving the efforts of Moravian missionary Christian Frederick Post to bring peace to the Ohio Valley in 1758.

Smucker, Barbara Claassen. *Henry's Red Sea* (1955). The dramatic escape of 1,000 Russian Mennonites from Berlin following World War II.

PONTIUS' PUDDLE
1980s: WOMEN BEGIN SMOKING IN GREATER NUMBERS--CLAIMING THE RIGHT TO KILL THEMSELVES.
DUBIOUS ACHIEVEMENT AWARDS
1990s: WOMEN BEGIN SERVING IN ACTIVE COMBAT -- EARNING THE OPPORTUNITY TO KILL OTHERS.
YOU'VE COME THE WRONG WAY, BABY!

PONTIUS' PUDDLE

AN EYE FOR AN EYE--

A PATRIOT FOR A SCUD--

A MIRAGE FIGHTER FOR A MIG-- AN APACHE COPTER FOR A T-72 TANK-

A NUCLEAR BLAST FOR A CHEMICAL ASSAULT--

THE NEW ESCALATE-OLOGY

BAKE SALE

"IT'LL BE A GREAT DAY
WHEN OUR SCHOOLS AND
CHURCHES HAVE ALL THE
MONEY THEY NEED AND THE
MILITARY HAS TO THROW A
BAKE SALE TO BUY A MISSILE."